TEACHER'S GUIDE

Discussion Manual for Student Relationships

Volume 1

Written by

Dawson McAllister

© Shepherd Productions, Inc., 1979
Moody Press Edition 1979

All rights reserved. No part of this book may be reproduced in any form without permission in writing from the publisher, except in the case of brief quotations embodied in critical articles or reviews.

ISBN 0-8024-2237-3

Printed in the United States of America

Introduction
Page 5

Steps to Better Understanding the Teacher's Guide
Page 6

The Bible, A Counseling Book

Lesson 1   Page 9
Lesson 2   Page 15

God's Will

Lesson 3   Page 22
Lesson 4   Page 26
Lesson 5   Page 30

Self Image

Lesson 6   Page 34
Lesson 7   Page 38
Lesson 8   Page 42

Loneliness

Lesson 9   Page 45
Lesson 10   Page 49

Parents

Lesson 11   Page 55
Lesson 12   Page 58
Lesson 13   Page 62
Lesson 14   Page 66

Sex

Lesson 15   Page 69
Lesson 16   Page 73
Lesson 17   Page 77

Dating

Lesson 18   Page 81
Lesson 19   Page 87
Lesson 20   Page 91

Love vs. Infatuation

Lesson 21   Page 95
Lesson 22   Page 99
Lesson 23   Page 102

Clearing the Mind

Lesson 24   Page 106
Lesson 25   Page 110

Temptation

Lesson 26   Page 114

Introduction

Congratulations! You have one of the highest priviledges given to teachers of God's Word--the privilege and responsibility of teaching God's answers to high school students.

You may be a pastor, a Sunday school teacher, a youth pastor, a Christian high school teacher, a volunteer youth leader or a parent. But whatever role you're in, God is using you to touch students' lives for Him. Can you think of any task more important than helping today's high school students grasp the solutions to their needs?

Never before have students needed God's answers for their lives more than today. Their thoughts and standards are being bombarded constantly by today's godless society. Every day students are being exposed to humanism, relativism, subjectivism, selfishness and hopelessness.

Christian students must know what God says about life's issues in order to withstand the evil pressures that surround them. You are a key person in helping them come to grips with God's answers; and you can help students obey God's answers through the power of the Holy Spirit on a day by day basis.

No one ever said teaching high school students was easy because it's not. They will challenge your resources, your knowledge and your faith. But praise God! Through His power, you <u>can</u> teach high school students.

It is our prayerful goal that this teacher's guide will help make you the best communicator that you can be to the youth that God has brought into your life.

Dawson McAllister and Rick Gilmore

Steps to Better Understanding the Teacher's Guide

In order to make your teaching efforts most effective, we strongly recommend that each student have a personal copy of the <u>Discussion Manual for Student Relationships, Volume 1</u>. This will result in more open discussion and deeper insights by your students.

Much like the discussion manual itself, this teacher's guide is designed with simplicity and relevancy. The following steps will help you better understand and use this teacher's guide.

I. You must study the <u>Discussion Manual For Student Relationships</u>.

The <u>Discussion Manual for Student Relationships</u> (hereafter referred to as the discussion manual) is essential in order to teach from this guide. Without the discussion manual, teaching from this guide would be impossible. In addition, the teacher's guide has been designed with the assumption that each student in your group has a copy of the discussion manual. Much of the actual lecture content is already contained in the discussion manual. We urge you to become so familiar with the discussion manual that you can teach from it with confidence.

The goal of this teacher's guide is to help you and your students better understand and put into practice the important concepts outlined in the discussion manual.

II. You must realize that there is more suggested material in each lesson than you probably can use in one session.

The writers of this teacher's guide strived to provide you with more tools than you really need. There are more than 50 hours of teaching material in the discussion manual. Therefore, it isn't necessary that you try to teach everything that is suggested. Students respond to different teaching techniques in different ways. Consequently, not every idea given in this teacher's guide will work best with your particular students.

III. Your creative ways may be better than those listed in the teacher's guide.

You probably have your own projects and illustrations to use with this material. No one knows your students or their situations like you do, so feel free to add your personal touch. That will get your creativity and your special gift of teaching directly involved.

IV. You must understand each component of the framework in order to effectively teach from this guide.

Our object is to keep this teacher's guide simple and practical in order to save you hours of research and preparation to teach the material. Therefore, the following is a description of the framework to be employed in each lesson.

A. Key Principles

In each lesson we have listed several key principles on which the study is based. It is your responsibility, in the power of the Holy Spirit, to communicate these principles so that your students can apply them to their lives. The remainder of the material in the teacher's guide is designed to embellish the key principles.

B. Key Verses

Scripture is vital in teaching any key principle to your students. From Scripture we get God's truths which always work. Consequently, we want to help you make those related key verses understandable and applicable.

Also, we provide supporting, cross reference verses that are not included in the discussion manual, so that you can teach from a broader perspective.

C. Key Questions

Asking key questions involves two important functions. One function is to invoke meaningful thought and discussion within your group. Secondly, questions stimulate your students to seek out important answers from Scripture. The majority of the questions listed in this guide are taken directly from the discussion manual. However, many other questions have been added where it was necessary to complete a thought or discussion.

D. Teacher Notes

The guideline most frequently provided for you is the teacher note, which gives you instructions on how to expand, clarify and interpret the material. Avoid overlooking the teacher note for the sake of expediency because each teacher note can also be an important resource of information on youth statistics, current trends and behavior.

E. Transparencies

In some cases a picture *is* worth a thousand words. So too, an overhead transparency can be an effective teaching tool. Even though the cartoons on the transparencies come from the discussion manual, we have found that when the cartoons are enlarged on a screen students tend to be more interested and attentive to the ideas being communicated. Nearly 80 transparencies are separately provided for this teacher's guide. However, the transparencies are <u>not</u> necessary for teaching from this guide. They are only provided as an addition tool for your teaching.
Shepherd Productions, Inc. for your order.

F. Projects

The best teacher is experience. Therefore, getting your students actively involved in the teaching process can prove to be your best assistant. We have suggested small group and individual projects such as discussion panels, role playing, writing exercises, etc., so that your students can teach themselves. Projects inserted occasionally will relieve you of the cumbersome task of lecturing and will add a new spark to the lesson.

G. Applications

Every high school student needs to have learning material applied to his life. From time to time we have inserted ways in which you can apply the material to your students' immediate life situations.

H. Illustrations

A personal example or an example of a well-known character can help your students associate an idea you are trying to communicate with a true life situation. Many illustrations are provided to add yet another dimension to your teaching and to your students' learning.

I. Transitions

It is very important that the principles you are teaching each week flow from one to the other. Therefore, we suggest certain ideas and statements on how to make the transition from one key principle to the next smooth and clear.

THE BIBLE, A COUNSELING BOOK
Lesson 1
Part 1 of Chapter 1
(pages 1-7)

Introduction:

To establish the great social and spiritual need among today's students is a very important way to begin teaching this study. The list of problems on page one is only a partial list of many more crises among young people. You may want to gather statistics, quotes and other sources to document the list. Or, you may want to do the following projects to prove the point.

Project A:

Pass out a sheet of paper to each student. Then have your students individually list what they think are the biggest problems on their campus. Give them three to five minutes to finish. Now, have each student share with you and the class what he has written. Now copy the problems on the overhead projector as they give them to you. Add spice to the discussion by asking each student to give examples of the problems he has listed. They will probably give you all the illustrations you need to prove the point that today's high school students are in great need.

Project B: *(optional)*

From the list of problems on page one, ask your students to rank the problems in order of severity--number one being the greatest problem and number twelve being the least.

Key Principles:

1. Through His Word, God has given the student guidelines on how to find true fulfillment.

2. The student is unfulfilled because <u>he ignores God</u> and His counsel on how to live.

Teacher Note: On page 2 of the discussion manual, Questions I and II will be included in Lesson One. Questions III and IV will be included in Lesson 2.

Key Principle 1:

Through His Word, God has given the student guidelines on how to find true fulfillment.

Transparency #1

8

Key Verses:

Jeremiah 9:23, 24

Teacher Note: It is important that you do not skim over these verses. In order to support principle one, Jeremiah 9:23, 24 must come alive and be applied to your students.

Key Questions:

1. What are the three areas you should not put your trust in, according to verse 23?
   (Answer: Have your students list these three areas on page 3 of their discussion manual: <u>WISDOM</u>, <u>MIGHT</u>, and <u>RICHES</u>.)

2. Why does God tell us not to trust in our own wisdom?
   (Answer A: Man apart from God cannot answer the important questions of life, such as:
   "Who am I?"
   "How did I get here?"
   "Where do I go when I die?"
   "What is the purpose to life?")
   (Answer B: Even though a person may know the wise thing to do in life, he does not have the power apart from God to do what he knows it is right to do.)

Supporting Verses: (Not trusting in man's wisdom.)

Isaiah 49:10
Romans 1:22 *professing to be wise, they became fools*
1 Corinthians 1:20, 21 *good*
Isaiah 49:10; 29:14

3. Why does God say, "Don't trust your own might"?
   (Answer: Man in all of his strength is totally frail in comparison to God.)

Illustration:

Try to illustrate a disaster when people were physically crushed and burned. Suggested illustration:
   The worse airplane disaster to date in America occurred in Chicago in May, 1979, when a large commercial airliner crashed and burned.

Supporting Verses: (Not trusting man's might.)

James 4:14 *life is a vapor - here today, gone tomorrow*
Isaiah 40:22-24
1 Samuel 20:3

4. Why does God tell us not to trust in our own riches?
   (Answer: Riches are only as good as our nation's economy. Need any more be said?)

Supporting Verses:

Proverbs 11:4
Ecclesiastes 6:2
James 1:11
James 5:1-3

Transition:

Just as verse 23 tells students what not to do, verse 24 tells students what they need to boast about to find true happiness.

Key Questions:

1. What does it mean to "know" God?
   (Answer: As you discuss page 4 of the discussion manual, it is important that you point out that knowing God is the art of seeking after, obeying, and imitating Him as well as communing with Him daily.)

2. What does it mean to understand God?
   (Answer: Again, it is important for you to describe characteristics of God from page 4 of the discussion manual. Understanding God is taking what we know about God and applying that to our lives.)

Supporting Verses:

David came to know and understand God's love and applied it to His life.
   See Psalms 31:21

David saw the faithfulness of God and applied it to his life.
   See Psalms 37:25

David applied the Lord's goodness to his life.
   See Psalms 27:13

Illustration:

You as a teacher need to give a personal illustration on how you have been able to apply what God offers to your life.

Transition:

In Jeremiah 9:24, God clearly tells us three areas which we can boast about and apply to our lives. As you can see on pages 4 & 5, the three areas are lovingkindness, justice and righteousness. All of these areas point to the fact that God has given us His counsel on how to live.

1. In Jeremiah 9:24 God says He acts in lovingkindness. Psalm 143:8 says, "Let me hear Thy lovingkindness in the morning; For I trust in Thee; Teach me the way in which I should walk; For to thee I lift up my soul." According to this verse, how does God show His lovingkindness?
   (Answer: Teacher, draw out from Psalm 143:8 that God shows us His lovingkindness by teaching us the way in which we should walk. In short, God gives us His loving counsel on how to live.)

Supporting Verses:

Psalms 143:8

2. Jeremiah 9:24 says that God also acts in justice. What does this mean, and how does God's justice apply to our lives?
   (Answer: As you can see on page 5, God acts in justice in order to deal with us in fairness and to teach us to respect the rights of others.)

   ### Supporting Verse:

   Proverbs 16:7

3. Jeremiah 9:24 says that God acts in righteousness. What does acting in righteousness mean?
   (Answer: As number three on the bottom of page five explains: God acting in righteousness means He does all things absolutely, morally right with no crookedness. His character is the standard for what is morally right. And since God acts only in the right way, the counsel which God gives is absolutely right.)

   ### Supporting Verses:

   Proverbs 2:7,8

Teacher Note: It is vital that you emphasize that God is _always_ right; therefore, His counsel on how to live is _always_ right.

Transition: (statement between key principles one and two)

If God loves man so much and has so much wise counsel on how to make man happy--what has happened so that the student finds his life in such chaos?

Transparency #2

Key Principle 2:

The student is unfulfilled because he ignores God and His counsel.

Key Verses:

    Romans 3:10,11

Teacher Note: It is important that you make these verses understood by your students. Jeremiah 9:24 says God is righteous, and He expects us to be righteous. But according to Romans 3:10, is anyone righteous? Understand?

Key Question:

    1. Jeremiah 9:24 says that we are to seek after God. But according to Romans 3:11, does anyone seek after God?
       (Answer: Because the student has ignored God's counsel, his life soon becomes problematic. Non-Christians may know they have problems but don't usually know why. See Proverbs 4:19.)

Transparency #3

    Key Verses:

        Proverbs 1:22,23

Project A:

Divide your students into two equal groups. Have group one answer the question, "What did the fool do to cause his life to turn into chaos?"
Have group two figure the consequences that the fool reaped for ignorning God's counsel.

Project B:

Go back to the list of 12 problems on page one of the discussion manual. List these problems on the overhead projector or the blackboard--some place where your group can read them. Now, list all of the Scriptural references you can think of beside each one to show where students with these problems have chosen to ignore God's counsel. Here are some helpful verses:

    loneliness--1 Corinthians 13
    friction in the home--Ephesians 6:1-3
    misuse of sex--1 Thessalonians 4:3-5
    sense of inferiority--Psalms 139:14,15
    bitterness and rebellion--Proverbs 17:11; Ephesians 4:29
    confusion concerning marriage--Ephesians 5:22,23
    temptation--James 1:13-15
    materialism--1 Timothy 6:9,10; 17-19
    mind pollution--Philippians 4:8
    hate--Titus 3:3; 1 John 4:20
    drugs and alcohol--1 Corinthians 6:18-20

Wrap Up/Application:

Explain to your students what the consequences are when we ignore God's counsel on how to live. Without His counsel, our lives will be in chaos. God has clearly put in Scripture His counsel on where we should and should not put importance. God vividly tells us if we ignore His counsel our lives will ultimately end up in chaos. These principles apply to Christians and non-Christians alike.

THE BIBLE, A COUNSELING BOOK
Lesson 2

Part 2 of Chapter 1
(pages 7-14)

Teacher Note: *This is not an easy lesson to teach. There are very few projects because there are many vital points which you need to establish with your students. You will need almost the entire time to lecture.*

Introduction/Review:

In order for this second lesson on "The Bible, A Counseling Book" to come together logically you will need to review lesson one. The best way to review is to ask your students quick questions about the previous lesson, such as:

*In what three areas does God tell us not to boast?
*Why did God warn us not to boast in wisdom?
*Why did God warn us not to boast in might?
*Why did God warn us not to boast in riches?
*What did God say we should boast about?
*What is one way God shows us His lovingkindness, justice, and righteousness?
(Answer: He gives us His counsel on how to live.)
*So, what has gone wrong with the student of today?
*What are some of the consequences of ignoring God and His counsel?

It is very important you begin this lesson by explaining to your class that God has answers to the predicaments in which students find themselves.

-God never fails.
-He loves us very much.
-God has a remedy for man's needs.

Key Principles:

1. *God has solved all our problems in Jesus Christ. True faith in Jesus Christ allows us peace with God and understanding of His counseling book. True faith gives us the power through the Holy Spirit to do what He counsels us to do.*

2. *God and His love have given us His counseling book full of insights to help us live a life of victory and joy. This counseling book is called the Bible.*

3. *God asks that we have the attitude of seeking...and attitude of forsaking sin...an attitude of humility with a teachable spirit... and an attitude of readiness to put into action His leading.*

Teacher Note: *The following concepts are discussed in the manual on page 8 under "God's Power, Love and Counsel." You need to elaborate on these explanations, therefore, we have provided the following concepts.*

Key Principle 1:

God has solved all problems in Jesus Christ. True faith in Him allows us peace with God and understanding of His counseling book. True faith gives us the power through the Holy Spirit to do what He counsels us to do.

A. When God opens the Christian's eyes to His counsel, it gives the Christian power to do what God directs him to do.

Key Verse:

2 Corinthians 9:8

Key Questions:

1. How much power does God give us to enable us to carry out His counsel?

2. Is there ever a time when God's power is not available to us?

B. When a Christian puts his faith in Jesus Christ, he automatically has peace with God.

Key Verse:

Romans 5:1

C. When a person comes to Christ, the Holy Spirit opens the believer's eyes to understanding and seeking God's counseling book.

Key Verse:

John 16:13

Supporting Verse:

1 John 2:27

Transition:

God has given us everything we need to have a life of peace and purpose. He has given us peace with Himself through Christ, a new desire to understand and seek His counsel, and power to do what He wants us to do.

Key Principle 2:

God and His love have given us His counseling book full of insights to help us live a life of victory and joy. This counseling book is called the Bible.

Key Verse:

2 Timothy 3:16

Teacher Note: *This verse is the keystone to the remainder of this series of relationships, but it is not easy to teach. Unless the student sees the power of the Bible in his life, he is not likely to take what you say seriously. Therefore, it will be important that you help your students fully understand 2 Timothy 3:16. It may help if you encourage all of your students to memorize it. These definitions of teaching, reproof, correction and training will go a little deeper than what is found on pages 8 and 9 of the discussion manual.*

Transparency #4

A. *Question:*

What does teaching mean?
(Answer: Teaching involves God revealing to us who He is and our response to Him as we walk down the road of life. Teaching includes doctrine as to who God is and what He has done in the person of Jesus Christ.

Example of God's teaching:

1 Peter 1:13-16

Transparency #5

B. *Question:*

What does reproof mean?
(Answer: Reproof is God exposing our sin through His Word and showing us that He is not pleased and that He expects us to get back on the right road.

Example of God's reproof:

James 4:1-4

Transparency #6

 C.   Question:

  What is correction?
  (Answer: God through His Word shows us how to get back on the right road with Him in order to restore us to an upright life style.

 Example of God's correction:

  Revelation 2:4,5

Transparency #7

 D.   Question:

  What is training in righteousness?
  (Answer: God through His Word teaches us ways to be disciplined in order to live a life that is pleasing to Him.

 Example of God's training in righteousness:

  Titus 2:11-14

Project (Optional):

If you are confident that you and your students clearly understand these four functions of the Word, then proceed with this project. Have your students turn to 1 Peter 5:1-9 and list the verses which directly apply to the four functions: teaching, reproof, correction and training in righteousness.

Project Key:

Verses 1-4 = Doctrine   Verse 5 = Reproof and Correction
Verses 6,7 = Correction   Verses 8,9 = Training in Righteousness

Transition:

God graciously gives us His wise counsel on how to live. He lays down attitudes that we must have in order to see His counsel work in our lives.

Key Principle 3:

God asks that we have the attitude of seeking...an attitude of forsaking sin...and attitude of humility and a teachable spirit...and an attitude of readiness to put into action His leading.

A. Attitude of Seeking.

Key Verses:

Proverbs 2:3-6

Project:

Have your students imagine that a famous, old ship was reported to have sunk somewhere in the sea. On that ship there were several million dollars worth of treasures, and they wanted to find that ship. Have them suggest some of the things they would do to locate the ship and recover its treasures. (Teacher: have your students suggest key ways to locate the sunken ship, the equipment they would need to get to it, and the methods of recovery.)

After completing that exercise, ask your students how they would seek after the mysteries of the Bible. Suggested ways would be through reading and studying other books, commentaries, dictionaries; studying the rewards and promises of the Bible; building up the desire and finding the time to study it; and listening to the preaching and teaching of others.

Teacher Note: Please stress that just as it would be difficult for any gold miner to find gold without the attitudes of patience, perseverance, diligence, determination, and in-depth searching, so it is with the believer. God's wisdom does not come from a superficial reading of the Bible, but from an intense and sincere study of His counsel. Otherwise, we would just use God, taking His rewards and answers, but spending little time loving Him and adjusting our lives to His ways and His holiness.

Supporting Verse:

2 Timothy 2:15

B. Attitude of Forsaking Sin.

Key Verse:

James 1:21

Key Questions:

1. What does "putting aside" mean?

2. What does "filthiness" mean?
   (Answer: Filthiness is the gross sin we have that disgusts the pure mind of God.)

3. What does "all that remains of wickedness" mean?
   (Answer: The remains of wickedness are the sins which we take lightly or accept, but are still evil in the sight of God [e.g. "white lies," unloving spirit, disrespect for authorities, etc.]).

Illustration:

Let's say you meet someone you are really attracted to. You decided to go on a date together. You probably would not show up in your oldest, smelliest clothes to seek to find out about that person. In a much greater way we offend God by coming to Him and His Word without stripping those sins from our lives that are filthy to Him and prevent Him from truly showing us His ways.

Supporting Verses:

Isaiah 1:11-16 (God is offended by people who will not deal with their sin, but who still come to Him.)

C. Attitude of Humility and Teachable Spirit.

Key Verse:

James 1:21

Key Questions:

1. What does "in humility receive the word" mean?
   (Answer: We must realize that God is the greatest teacher and counselor. In order to come before Him, we need to have an attitude like a willing child who wants to learn.)

2. Why is it harmful to come to God's Word with a rebellious attitude?
   Answer: In essence, we are telling God that we know more than He does, and that His ideas and ways don't mean much to us. In other words, we can take them or leave them.)

Teacher Note: Throughout the following weeks, you are going to teach some things your students may not like to hear; nonetheless, it is true counsel from God's Word. When God tells us things we do not want to hear, normally our response will tell us whether we are truly coming to God's counsel in humility.

Supporting Verse:

2 Thessalonians 2:13

D. Attitude of Readiness to put into Action God's Leading.

Key Verses:

James 1:22-25

Key Questions:

1. What does a person do to himself when he hears the Word, understands it, but does not act on it?
   (Answer: He deludes himself, which simply means that he is faked out by false reasoning; he thinks that simply hearing the Word will change his life, when in reality he also must obey it to avoid delusion.)

Transparency #8

Project:

Teacher, plan this project before your group meets, with one of your more secure, popular students to avoid possible embarrassment or ridicule. You will need a mirror for this exercise. When it's time for this project, have the student stand far away from the mirror facing it as you hold it or as it is hung on a wall. Now have the student describe distinct features about himself before the group. Next, have the student slowly walk towards the mirror continually describing features or fallacies that he can see. The closer he comes to the mirror, the more detail he should describe about the way he looks, until he is right up to the mirror describing the minor details of his face. Then relate to your students from this exercise that God's Word is a mirror. The closer we get to God through reading the Bible, the more He reveals to us areas that we need to work on to improve ourselves.

Wrap Up/Conclusion:

Now would be an excellent time to challenge your students to pray that God would give them the right attitudes as you proceed to teach this course. Challenge them to silently ask God to give them:
    a. an attitude of seeking.
    b. an attitude of forsaking sin.
    c. an attitude of humility and teachable spirit.
    d. an attitude of readiness to put God's leading into action.

GOD'S WILL
Lesson 3

Part 1 of Chapter 2
(pages 17-23)

Introduction:

Teacher, the following three lessons, which cover the importance of knowing God's will, are very strategic to the spiritual growth of your students. Many high school students, because they are not spiritually mature, do not recognize that God wants to be actively involved in the details of their daily lives. Therefore, these students are in the habit of making important decisions without first seeking God's counsel. This explains why the faith of some students becomes dead and theoretical rather than alive and practical. In these lessons, your goal is to teach your students a Biblical framework in which they will be able to discern God's will in making the right decisions.

Project:

Pass out a sheet of paper to each student. Ask each student to think about instances in the last two years of his life when he needed to know God's will. Now, have the students list them. On the other side of the paper, have them list some of the crucial decisions they will need to make in the next five years. (Examples of some decisions are listed on page 17 of the discussion manual.) They will need to save their papers for reference later in the session.

Illustration:

Teacher, as you begin this lesson, be sure to explain to your students that doing God's will is the single, most important thing they will ever do in their lives.

Jesus Christ, our great example, also sought out God's will. Jesus showed us how to live a life that is pleasing to the Father. Christ was driven by the key desire to do the Father's will at all times. He said in John 6:38, "For I have come down from heaven, not to do My own will, but to do the will of Him who sent Me." When Jesus entered this world, He had no selfish intentions. He only wanted to do the perfect will of the Father. Jesus said in John 4:34, "My food is to do the will of Him who sent Me, and to accomplish His work." Jesus still ate food, but He was saying that He could not survive without doing the Father's will--to accomplish what He was commanded to do by God. Jesus, also, proved that He only wanted to do the will of the Father when He went into the Garden of Gethsemane. Matthew 26:39 says, "And He went a little beyond them, and fell on His face and prayed, saying, 'My Father, if it is possible, let this cup pass from Me; yet not as I will, but as Thou wilt.'"

Key Principles:

1. You must realize that God <u>does</u> <u>have</u> a will for your life.

2. If you want to know God's will, you must have an attitude of acceptance of His ways and His plans.

Teacher Note: Many students believe that God is only in the heavenlies. God personally caring for their lives is hard for them to accept. Therefore, you must strive to make the following three lessons as practical as possible.

Project:

Have each student read aloud the list of areas in which he needed to know God's will during the past two years.

Key Principle 1:

You must realize that God <u>does</u> <u>have</u> a will for your life.

Transparency #9

Key Verses:

Matthew 6:26
Psalms 32:8
Proverbs 3:5,6
Matthew 10:29,30

Teacher Note: When referring to Matthew 6:26; 10:29-30, stress the kind of detail God is concerned about, like the birds of the air and the hair on the human head. Point out how much more important we are in God's sight than birds or hair.

Key Questions:

1. According to Psalm 32:8, why does God want us to trust Him with all our hearts?

2. From Proverbs 3:5-6, why does God want us to trust Him with all our hearts?

3. In finding out the best way we should do things, why does God say we should not lean on our own understanding?

4. What does it mean, "In all your ways acknowledge Him?"

5. Would God ask us to trust Him completely if He was going to let us down?

6. What does it mean, "He will make your paths straight?"

Transparency #10

Teacher Note: *To conclude this first principle, stress that God is not playing a game of hide-and-go-seek as we discover His will. He doesn't hide His will behind a bush and say, "Now go and find it; I'll tell you when you're getting close." <u>God never plays any kind of game with us</u>.*

Transition:

If we want to know God's will for our lives, we must realize that He has a special will for us. But simply knowing that God has a will for us is not enough. God expects us to go further.

Key Principle 2:

If you want to know God's will, you must have an attitude of acceptance of His ways and His plans.

Transparency #11

Key Verses:

Romans 12:1,2

A. Explanation of Romans 12:1,2. Teacher, stress that obedience to God is necessary in order to be in His will. Also, by being obedient we allow God the freedom to direct other areas of our lives besides just the major decisions. The last part of verse two ("that you may prove what the will of God is...") is the result of obeying the commands previously listed in verses one and two. The two commands in verses one and two are: 1) Present your bodies as a living sacrifice; 2) Do not be conformed to this world.

Key Questions:

1. What does it mean, "present your bodies as a living and holy sacrifice...?"

2. What does it mean, "And do not be conformed to this world, but be transformed...?"

B. Here are two tests to see if we have the right attitude to be in God's will.

Teacher Note: *The following exercises are an attempt to make the doctrine of Romans 12:1,2 more practical.*

First Test: (Your goal, teacher, is to help your students recognize that their attitudes must be submissive to God's will. If their attitudes are not submissive to God's leading, then they are just using God as a divine Santa Claus.) Are you obeying the parts of God's will you already know? If not, why should God continue to tell you what is the rest of His will? (Page 21 of the discussion manual lists areas God shows us of His will. You may want to add to this list.)

Supporting Verse:

John 14:21

Teacher Note: *Point out that not to be in submission to the will of God is to grieve the Holy Spirit, who guides us into God's will. This would be like stepping on the gas pedal and brake pedal of a car at the same time.*

Second Test: Are you willing to accept God's will for your life even before you know it?

Transparency #12

Key Verses:

Mark 8:34,35

Supporting Verse:

Romans 8:32

Teacher Note: *You need to understand that probably some of your students have not come to accept the lordship of Jesus Christ in their lives. To accept God's way as the happiest and most perfect way is still very hard for them. Your students may tend to believe that they should have the option of knowing the Lord's will in their lives before saying yes or no to it. You need to share with them gently and lovingly that God does not want them to have this attitude. To have the attitude of wanting to choose whether to accept or reject God's will is not denying ourselves and thus being true disciples of Christ. Your students need to realize that God is not the big "rip-off" in the sky, as explained at the top of page 23 in the discussion manual.*

Wrap Up/Application:

Challenge each student in the room to share areas, listed at the start of the session, in which they need to know God's will. Next, ask them to honestly ask themselves, "Am I in God's will right now?"

Stress that it is important for them to know what college to go to, or what job to take or who to marry. But point out that before they can know these things, they must put every area of their lives on the altar for God.

GOD'S WILL
Lesson 4

Part 2 of Chapter 2
(pages 23-29)

Introduction:

With the exception of chapter one of the discussion manual, chapter two is, perhaps, the most difficult to teach and to understand. Therefore, you should do a thorough review of the previous lesson by listing the key principles and their related verses on an overhead projector or a blackboard. Review each principle carefully with your class. Don't worry about taking time for review, as the repetition will help your students to learn. Also, reviewing the previous lesson will give you the proper framework in which to begin today's lesson. The reason you need to review is because no single principle on how to know God's will can provide the complete answer. All principles throughout the three lessons on God's will are directly related to one another. Your students need to recognize that the answers all fit together into one formula for knowing God's will, rather than seeing each answer as a separate entity that works on its own. Review, therefore, is important.

Key Principles:

1. A large part of God's plan for our lives is already revealed for us in the Bible.

2. Even though God is deeply concerned about us and about revealing His will for our lives, there are some aspects of His plan that He will reveal only <u>one</u> <u>day</u> <u>at</u> <u>a</u> <u>time</u>.

3. God directs us to His will through prayer.

Key Principle 1:

A large part of God's plan for our lives is already revealed for us in the Bible.

Transparency #13

Key Verse:

Psalm 119:24

Key Questions:

1. Where did David turn first when he needed counsel?

2. Why did he call God's testimonies in His Word as such a friend?

Teacher Note: Be sure you understand and can clearly communicate the following two aspects of God's will: His will for specific areas in our lives not found in the Bible; and, His will for our lives that applies to all Christians. (Further explanation of this is found in the discussion manual on page 24.)

Inform your students that they can save a lot of time and emotional effort by going to God's Word first where He has already put forth a portion of His will for them.

On pages 24 and 25 of the discussion manual are five examples of areas God has already revealed to Christians. Read and briefly discuss these examples with your class.

Project:

From the last lesson each student should have listed at least one area in which he is seeking God's will. Split up your class into small groups of three or four students, and give each group the assignment of finding any scriptural references that relate to just one area in which each student is seeking God's will. (You may want to search out before the project some verses in case your students cannot think of any.)

Transition:

Some people can find the answers to God's will for their lives in Scripture; others must wait for God to reveal His will to them. So, it is important for us to know how God does reveal His will for our lives.

Key Principle 2:

Even though God is deeply concerned about us and about revealing His will for our lives, there are some aspects of His plan that He will reveal only <u>one</u> <u>day</u> <u>at</u> <u>a</u> <u>time</u>.

Transparency #14

Key Verses:

John 16:12
Matthew 6:34
Psalm 27:14

Teacher Note: Tell your students that God may wait until the very last moment to reveal what He wants them to do, or He may reveal only a small percentage of His plan on a daily basis. Assure your students that there is no need to get frustrated over waiting for God to act. Share with your students that God is not playing games with them, but actually He is looking out for their best interests, and He is helping them to grow as Christians.

Key Question:

1. Why does God tell us only small portions of His will on a daily basis?
   (Answer: If God told us everything about our futures, it would really burden us down today. This would make functioning in life nearly impossible.)

Application:

"What if..." questions... (Teacher, ask these questions to individuals in your class to spark discussion and prove the point of why God reveals His will patiently.)

1. What if God told _(girl)_ she was going to marry a doctor in five years? What kind of complications would that cause her?

2. What if God revealed to _(guy)_ he would be single the rest of his life? What kind of pressure would that cause him?

3. What if God told _(guy)_ he would be the pastor of a church with 2,000 members? What would be his thoughts and how would he react?

4. What if God told you that at age 21 you would die? What kind of problems would that cause you now?

Key Question:

1. What might God be doing when He does not tell us His will for a situation until the very last moment?
   (Answer: He might be showing us that His power is just as good at the very last moment as it is over a long period of time.)

Illustration:

God want us to learn to focus our eyes just on Him. We tend to give more attention to the plan for our lives, so we quit seeking Him with earnestness.

Key Principle 3:

God directs us to His will through prayer.

Key Verses:

Luke 6:12,13

Illustration:

Prayer is a truly amazing vehicle for knowing God's will. Through prayer we petition God for answers to our questions and for fulfillment of our needs. Prayer also enables us to open up ourselves so that God can speak to us through His Holy Spirit. The best time for God to gain access to our thoughts is when we are involved in deep serious prayer. Because we have a desire for God to reveal His will to us, we need to spend much time in prayer.

Illustration:

Example: Jesus Christ. The fact that Jesus did spend time in prayer even though He was God in the flesh and knew all things might seem peculiar. But Jesus laid aside His rights to be God so that we might be totally dependant on the Father to know His will. This truth is evident in Luke 6:12,13 (key verses) when Jesus had to choose His 12 disciples. Although He had spent time with them, Jesus still prayed all night in order to receive God's counsel.

Application:

If Jesus spent the entire night in prayer, how much time do we need to spend in prayer seeking God's will. For an example of the early church turn to Acts 13:2,3. From this passage we learn that the early church was in such an infant stage that every decision had an impact on the eternal growth of the church.

Two important points to notice:
1. *Men were in prayer when God spoke to them.*
2. *Even after the Holy Spirit told the apostles what to do, they prayed more. Why did they continue to pray?*

Wrap Up/Application:

After explaining the section entitled "Spend Five Minutes" found at the top of page 30 in the discussion manual, you may want to conclude the lesson with this prayer project.

Divide the class into pairs, and have each partner share with the other one of their needs for knowing God's will. Now have each pair pray together for each other's need.

GOD'S WILL
Lesson 5

Part 3 of Chapter 2
(pages 30-34)

Introduction:

You should review the key principles of the previous two lessons on knowing God's will. A good way to review is to have your students use their discussion manuals to tell you what key principles have been discussed. Never hesitate to review or be hasty when reviewing. Helping your students retain what already has been covered is more important than trying to finish all of the material in the manual. In addition, you may want to ask your students this question of the five key principles studied thus far: "Which one of the key principles means the most to you? Why?"

Key Principles:

1. We are wise when we get counsel from those who love us and who are are actively seeking God's will for their own lives.

2. At times, God uses circumstances to point us in the direction we should go.

3. When we are under submission to Jesus Christ and controlled and empowered by the Holy Spirit, we can accept by faith that our reasoning in the matter is sound and led by God.

Key Principle 1:

We are wise when we get counsel from those who love us and who are actively seeking God's will for their own lives.

Key Verse:

Proverbs 11:14

Transparencies #15 & #16

Supporting Verses:

Psalms 1:1
Proverbs 12:15

Teacher Note: You should clarify why we need to seek wise counsel when discerning God's will for our lives. When you do this, keep in mind that most students act impulsively, meaning that they let their emotions dictate how they should behave before considering all the facts.

Illustration:

Give a personal illustration of a time when you made a decision before getting wise counsel and then paid for the wrong decision. Now, ask your students to share an incident when they did not seek wise counsel, and ended up suffering because of a wrong decision.

Key Questions:

1. How can we make wrong decisions without proper counsel?

2. Why does God want us to have many counselors?

Teacher Note: Read Psalms 1:1 to your students and then emphasize that they need to get counsel from other Christians.

Project:

Pass out a sheet of paper to each student and have him list four or five counselors he would refer to in seeking God's counsel for a decision. Next, have him explain why he would choose these particular people.

Teacher Note: You need to warn your students that if they feel strongly about a decision they are close to making, but refuse to seek counsel because of the fear of what the counselor may say, they are making a big mistake!

Supporting Verse:

Proverbs 12:15

Key Principle 2:

At times, God uses circumstances to point us in the direction we should go.

Teacher Note: You need to be careful when teaching this principle because most people use circumstances as the key indicator for God's will. Do not over-emphasize this principle in relation to the other key principles.

Key Verses:

Romans 1:13
1 Corinthians 16:8,9

Project:

Write both key verses (Romans 1:13 and 1 Corinthians 16:8,9) on an overhead projector or a blackboard. Now have the students write down on a sheet of *paper some of the circumstances God allowed them to go through in order to keep him at the center of God's will.*

Illustration:

Share with the class an example in your life when circumstances showed you what to do.

Teacher Note: *An important warning about circumstances in on page 32 of the discussion manual under "Another Warning?" Read this to your class before teaching the next key principle.*

Transition:

At the top of page 33 in the discussion manual are seven "if" situations in discerning God's will. Read these to your class. Now, stress that after these "if" situations are completed, <u>then</u> key principle three can be implemented.

Key Principle 3:

When we are under submission to Jesus Christ and controlled and empowered by the Holy Spirit, we can accept by faith that our reasoning in the matter is sound and led by God.

Key Verses:

2 Timothy 1:7
Philippians 2:13
Psalms 37:23,24

Teacher Note: *Inform your students that there comes a time when a decision simply needs to be made and then carried out by heading in that direction. Tell your students that if they submit themselves to the key principles taught in these three lessons, they can be confident in making the right decisions.*

Project:

"God Wants You To Use Your Mind!" An example of this project is illustrated on page 33 of the discussion manual. You will recall from the first lesson that your students wrote down decisions in which they needed to know God's will. Have each student write down that decision on a new sheet of paper. Now, have them list below the decision and the pros and cons related to it.

Teacher Note: *Point out that while some students are impulsive in making decisions, other students procrastinate for a long time. This, also, is a mistake.*

Key Verses:

    Psalms 37:23,24

Transparency #17

    Key Questions:

        1. Who is actively involved in the man's situation?

        2. What does God do to assure us that our decision will not lead us to disaster?

Teacher Note: Some of your students may feel that just because they want to go in a certain direction and are excited about it, it must mean that it is not God's will. Relieve them of this guilt by sharing Psalms 37:4,5.

Wrap Up/Application:

Have your students pray aloud or to themselves by repeating the following prayer as you read it one sentence at a time:

"God, I thank You that You have a will for my life."

"God, I ask that I might have an attitude of acceptance of Your ways and Your plans."

"God, I thank You for already revealing a large portion of Your will for me in the Bible."

"God, I realize that You may reveal Your will for my life only one day at a time."

"God, I thank You for the way You will direct me through prayer."

"God, I thank You for other Christians You will use to give me wise counsel."

"God, I thank You for circumstances that You will use to direct me."

"God, I thank You that I can accept by faith my own reasoning in matters when I am under submission to Jesus and empowered by Your Holy Spirit."

SELF IMAGE
Lesson 6

Part 1 of Chapter 3
(pages 39-47)

Introduction:

Explain to your students that outside the need for knowing Christ as personal Savior, a poor self image is probably the most common problem of everyone. Self image affects every human being, whether he is attractive or not.

Teacher, has there ever been a time in your life when you have struggled with self image? Perhaps an effective way to begin this series of lessons on self image would be by giving a personal illustration of any past problems you have had with your self image.

Transparency #18

Project:

Give each student a sheet of paper and ask him to answer the questions on page 39 in the discussion manual in two sentences, as honestly as possible. Also, add this question to the list: If there is one feature of your physical appearance you could change, what would you change? Next have your students put check marks by the features they can relate to, listed on page 40 in the discussion manual. (If your students do not have their own copies of the discussion manual, you will have to list these features on an overhead projector or a blackboard.)

Transparency #19

Teacher Note: Point out to your students that having a good self image means accepting themselves. If they have a poor attitude toward accepting themselves, it can affect their relationships with other people, with themselves and with God.

Key Principles:

1. The world is so caught up in beauty and ability that it can deeply affect our own willingness to accept the ability and appearance God has given us.

2. We can have a much healthier view of ourselves if we look at our appearance and abilities the way God looks at them.

Key Principle 1:

The world is so caught up in beauty and ability that it can deeply affect our own willingness to accept the ability and appearance God has given us.

Teacher Note: On page 42 of the discussion manual is a list of eight questions that show how much the world is hung-up on the cult of the beautiful. Ask your students these eight questions and challenge them to give illustrations from their own lives so they relate to the questions.

Key Verses:

Ephesians 4:17-19 (Your students need to recognize that this verse provides the answer to our world and its future. They also need to see that man has ignored God's standards for true beauty, and has created his own. This new standard of beauty consists of the outward and sensual beauty of man. The problem with worshipping physical beauty is that it soon fades away; therefore, no one can always live up to this man-made standard.

Key Questions:

1. Why does man, apart from God, seem to put so much emphasis on appearance?

2. Where have wrong values led those who ignore God?

3. What does this statement mean, "being darkened in their understanding, excluded from the life of God?"

4. What has happened to the godless man?

Teacher Note: The concepts found on pages 43 and 44 of the discussion manual need to be clearly taught to your students. Please stress, while teaching these, that God does not want Christians to think like the world thinks. If Christians do think as the world does, then they will be just as frustrated as the world. God gives Christians a remedy for this frustration in Romans 12:2. Read this verse to your class.

Supporting Verses:

Romans 12:2
1 John 2:15,16

Project:

Get some copies of the popular magazines of the day (e.g. Seventeen, Glamour, Mademoiselle, Esquire, Time, Teen Beat). Next, cut out the advertisements and articles that deal with a person's self image. In class show the ads and articles to your students and have them analyze the ads and articles. As they analyze, point out how often an advertisement will play on the fear of failure/rejection or how the ad puts forth a stereotype of a person that few people will ever reach.

Transition:

God warns us not to think of our self images like the non-Christians think of theirs. We can be free from a poor self image when we begin to look at ourselves the way God looks at us.

Key Principle 2:

We can have a much healthier view of ourselves if we look at our appearance and abilities the way God looks at them. He does not put prime importance on physical appearance or strength.

Key Verse:

1 Samuel 16:7

Key Question:

1. Why does God put more importance on the inner man than on the physical appearance?
   (Answer: A man's frame or physical body is only a temporal item. It weakens and eventually dies with the passing of time; yet, man's inward soul or personality will live forever.

Supporting Verses:

2 Corinthians 4:18
Proverbs 31:30

Teacher Note: The word "vain" in Proverbs 31:30 means, "here today, gone tomorrow."

Transparency #20

(Answer B: The physical frame is limited in changing. Man, when born, is limited in his ability to change the basic aspects of his physical body. However, man has the ability to change his personality and character. God sees inward development as having much greater importance than physical.)

Supporting Verses:

Matthew 6:27-29
Psalm 147:10, 11

Wrap Up/Application:

   As you conclude today's lesson, stress to your students that the majority of their peers at school think the wrong way about the beauty and appearance of man. But, assure your students that just because their close friends and peers think like the world, this should not force them to think the same way. Warn your students that if they allow themselves to think like the world, they will begin to stress their own self images.

   Also, tell your students that the next two lessons will be covering more of self image.

SELF IMAGE
Lesson 7

Part 2 of Chapter 3
(pages 47-55)

Introduction:

For this lesson's introduction, ask review questions on the previous lesson like:
- Why do people have such a poor self-image?
- Why are the world's standards on beauty so frustrating?
- God does not put prime importance on physical beauty. Why?

Teacher Note: Tell your class that during this lesson and the next lesson you will be discussing God's standards for true beauty.

Key Principles:

1. God focuses on the inner person, rather than the external; therefore, His desire for us is to have real inner beauty.

2. God was actively involved in the creation of our bodies for His own purposes, and He is still participating in our development.

3. God wants us to have a healthy countenance; therefore, we can have an effect on how we look.

(handwritten note: Summary)

Key Principle 1:

God focuses on the inner person, rather than the external, therefore, His desire for us is to have real inner beauty.

Transparency #21

Key Verses:

1 Peter 3:3,4

Key Questions:

1. What are some characteristics of inner beauty?
   (Answers: Everyone is eligible to have it. It crosses all age barriers. It cannot be bought, yet.... It is priceless. It is eternal. Jesus had it. God wants you to have it. You would be a unique person to have it.)

2. What is inner beauty?
   (Answer: Inner beauty is the inner characteristic that the Holy Spirit develops within Christians to please God, such as: peace, patience, kindness, goodness, gentleness, faithfulness, love, joy and self-control.

3. Why are the characteristics of inner beauty so precious in the sight of God?

4. If inner beauty (i.e., love, joy, peace) is so priceless, why don't more people seek after it?

Project:

Pass out a sheet of paper to each student. Have your students write a paragraph description on what they think of one person they know who has an attractive physical appearance, but who has very little inner beauty. Next, have your students describe what they think of another person they know who is not particularly physically attractive, but who has many qualities of inward beauty. After your students have completed their two descriptions, get them to describe on paper how they now see the second person's physical appearance after experiencing their inner beauty. If some students wish to share their descriptions, have them read the paragraphs before the group.

Supporting Verses:

Isaiah 40:30,31

Teacher Note: Stress to your class that they would be wise to spend more time and emotional energy developing the inner beauty God counts valuable, rather than worrying over the world's way of boosting self-image through appearance, which ends in frustration.

Transition:

God wants us to know that He thinks our inner beauty is more important than outward beauty. He also wants us to know that He was directly involved with our creation.

Transparency #22

Key Principle 2:

God was actively involved in the creation of our bodies for His own purposes, and He is still participating in our development.

Key Verses:

Psalm 139:13-15

Project:

Place the following four erroneous views on an overhead projector or blackboard. High school students tend to think their personal creation fits into one of these views: (1) Looks were created more or less by accident or chance; (2) God was too big and too busy to personally have designed looks; (3) God gave some people a "raw deal" with looks, while others were more "blessed" by God; or (4) God is finished with the development or looks, and He will not do anything more with looks.

Next, ask your students to answer the following questions aloud.
1. What does Psalm 139:13-15 say about two of these four erroneous views?
2. How does James 3:17 answer one of these views?
3. In Ephesians 2:10, what does "we are" mean?
   (Answer: God is still working with us; He is not finished with us yet.)

Explain to your students that God is not through with the development and designing of our frames. We have a purpose to fulfill so that people will give God the glory and praise for our inner and outer beauty.

To complete this project, have your students thank God in prayer for wonderfully designing them. Have them look for the great plan for their lives He has in store.

Key Principle 3:

God wants us to have a healthy countenance; therefore, we can have an effect on how we look.

Key Verse:

Psalm 43:5

Supporting Verse:

Proverbs 13:15

Key Questions:

1. What is a countenance?
   (Answer: The expression of the face which reveals the inner condition of the heart.)

2. According to Psalm 43:5, how does David describe God in relationship to David's countenance?
   (Answer: God is the health of my countenance.)

3. What causes an <u>unhealthy</u> countenance?
   (Answers: Anger and bitterness, Proverbs 25:23; sin, Isaiah 3:9; pride and irreverance, Psalm 10:4; guilt, Psalm 32:3.)

Transparency #23

Teacher Note: *Explain that the Bible indicates a countenance can be healthy or unhealthy, depending on what is inside the heart. Therefore, whether our countenance is healthy or not depends on us--we can control the state of our countenance.*

Project:

Get about ten pictures of people who do not have healthy countenances. You may want to go to your local police department for picture posters of wanted criminals, or seek magazine or newspaper pictures of individuals you sense have unhealthy countenances. Once you have the pictures, show them to your class. Ask your students what they think are the expressions on the person's face. Next, ask them why they think these people have unhealthy countenances.

Now, ask your students how they felt towards a person they saw or knew who had a bitter countenance, and ask them to explain the difference of how they felt when they saw or knew someone who had an expression of love and acceptance. And to complete the project, ask your students to tell you what kinds of sins, in particular, may cause an unhealthy countenance. (Some examples might be: misuse of drugs and alcohol, rebellion toward authority or rebuke by authority, fear of others, frustration from not getting desires, misuse of sex, rejection and deception.)

Wrap Up/Application:

Conclude by telling your students that God wants us to know that when we have a clear conscience, a heart set on pleasing God, and a willingness to be gracious in accepting others, <u>then</u> we will have a healthy countenance.

When our countenances are healthy, we have a certain shine and warmth to our faces that will attract others to us. And when we seek God and His wise counsel, we can have that healthy countenance.

God gives us His wise counsel in Ecclesiastes 8:1: "Who is like the wise man? Who knows the explanation of things? Wisdom brightens a man's face and changes its hard appearance."

SELF IMAGE
Lesson 8

Part 3 of Chapter 3
(pages 55-60)

Introduction:

In order that the "Self Image" chapters have continuity, you will need to briefly summarize the previous two lessons. Do not underestimate the validity of review, as students are able to learn and retain more through repetition. One good method of review would be to write the key principles of the "Self Image" chapters on an overhead projector or blackboard. Or, you could direct the students back to the key principles in their discussion manuals. This will allow the students to follow along while you read and explain the key principles.

Key Principles:

1. One way we can overcome the problem of accepting ourselves is to let God use our weaknesses as motivators so He can work through us more.

2. We should realize how God desires us to view our abilities and talents.

Key Principle 1:

One way we can overcome the problem of accepting ourselves is to let God use our weaknesses as motivators so He can work through us more.

Key Verse:

1 Corinthians 1:27

(Explanation: God has put into effect a certain rule that He loves to apply in our lives. If we keep this rule in mind, we can turn our inferiorities into strengths through God's power. See "Rule" at the top of page 56 in the discussion manual.)

Key Question:

1. According to 1 Corinthians 1:27, what two things does God use to show His greatness?
   (Answer: Be sure to refer to the boxes on page 56 of the discussion manual titled: "What are the foolish..." and "What are the weak...".)

Transparency #24

Project:

Give each student a sheet of paper, and ask them to mentally place themselves in the following situation. If they were to set a goal of speaking to 2,000 students on other campuses about Christ, what kinds of personal

weaknesses would arise in them before they accomplished their goal? Now have your students list these areas on the paper.

After your students have listed their areas of weakness, inform them that these are the very things that can help them to trust God more.

TWO EXAMPLES OF THIS PRINCIPLE:

1. Jesus Christ

Isaiah 53:2 says that Jesus was not attractive in the sense of what the world thinks is attractive. Yet, people of the world flocked to Jesus. Why?

He had tremendous inner beauty - Mark 6:34
He spoke with authority - Matthew 7:28,29
He depended upon the Father totally - Matthew 28:18
His message went beyond superficial issues - Mark 13:31

Teacher Note: Your students need to know that these four areas in which Christ was strong, are also areas in which they can be strong.

2. Apostle Paul

2 Corinthians 12:7-12 states that Paul had a thorn in the flesh. Some Bible scholars say he had epilepsy, and others contend he had an ugly eye disease. Whatever the ailment, it marred Paul's appearance. (Also, see Galatians 4:13, 14) Paul prayed three times that God would remove the ailment, but it did not leave Him.

In verse ten of 2 Corinthians 12, Paul applies the principle that weakness can be made strong and perfect.

Transition:

God wants our weaknesses to motivate us more. But He wants us to view our strengths, abilities and talents in the proper way.

Key Principle 2:

We should realize how God desires us to view our abilities and talents.

Teacher Note: Be sure not to cause anyone in your class to have guilty feelings for being a good athlete or attractive or brilliant. share, however, that all of these qualities are good when they are held in the proper perspective.

Key Question:

1. What is the proper perspective when we know we have special talents or attractiveness?
   (Answer: In comparision to knowing Jesus Christ, good looks, athletic talents and intelligence are secondary at best.)

Key Verses:

Philippians 3:46-48

Key Questions:

1. According to Philippians 3:4b-8, could Paul really trust in his own abilities?

2. How does Paul compare his earthly accomplishments to his knowledge of Christ?

Transparency #25   (Leave transparency on screen through rest of lesson.)

Project:

Pass out another sheet of paper to each student. Have them write down their strong points (good looks, common sense, plays basketball well, liked by everyone, etc.). After they have finished listing their good qualities, have your students write out the verse Colossians 3:17 over the list.

Wrap Up/Application:

Stress to your students that all of them have strengths and weaknesses. But whenever they see themselves from God's perspective, their weaknesses can become strengths and their present strengths can be put into proper perspective.
Perhaps you should read this to your class:
"You are part of the world into which God sent His Son, Jesus Christ. God's love for you motivated Him to send Jesus. Isn't it great to know that God feels you are that important and valuable!? You also need to realize how important you are to God by giving yourself back to Him for His purpose."

(Optional)

You might want to review the past three lessons and their projects, and challenge your students to give all of their self-image to God.

LONELINESS
Lesson 9
Part 1 of Chapter 4
(pages 63-70)

Introduction:

Loneliness is such a crippling feeling of isolation and failure that few high school students want to admit that they are lonely or want to get help. Yet, loneliness is a condition just about everyone of your teens is experiencing or will experience in the future.

Therefore, the more you can get your students to discuss the subject of loneliness, the more you can help them in the power of the Holy Spirit.

Transparency #26

Project:

Split your class into groups of five or smaller. Give each student three minutes to share with the other group members <u>the loneliest circumstance they can remember</u>, <u>how they felt at the time</u>, and <u>how they got out of the situation</u>.

Next, have each group come up with two different examples of loneliness. On page 63 of the discussion manual, there are seven examples of loneliness. From the seven, have each group pick the example that fits closest to their examples.

Teacher Note: You may want to ask the class why loneliness is such a devastating feeling. One answer might be that loneliness cuts down into some of our deepest needs. These needs include the overwhelming desire to love, to be loved, and to be held in high esteem by at least one other person.

Key Principles:

1. The first step out of loneliness is to stop worrying about your immediate situation, mentally get hold of yourself, then move ahead to positive action

2. The second step out of loneliness is to be honest with yourself and with God, and to seek friendship and emotional support of other people.

Key Principle 1:

The first step out of loneliness is to stop worrying about your immediate situation, mentally get hold of yourself, then move ahead to positive action.

Transparency #27

Key Verses:

Psalms 42:3-5

Teacher Note: Explain that a lonely person overreacts and can go into an emotional tailspin which leads him to frustration. On top of page 65 of the discussion manual is a list of some of the symptoms of loneliness. (You may wish to list the symptoms on an overhead projector or blackboard.) Stress that God never intended man to be caught in this kind of a vicious circle.

Supporting Verses:

Matthew 11:28 (see page 65 of the discussion manual for three good
 questions that will relate this verse to loneliness.)
Psalm 42:3-5 (Psalm 42 is the best chapter in the Bible written
 about loneliness.)

Key Questions:

1. According to Psalm 42, what were some of the circumstances that cause the man to be so emotionally upset and lonely?

2. What did the psalmist do to begin to see victory over his pained emotions?

Teacher Note: Stress to the students that these are some statements they can tell themselves that will help get them out of lonelinesss. The statements are on page 66 of the disucssion manual.

Transparency #28

Transition:

Not only must you be your own counselor by stopping yourself from going into an emotional tailspin, but you must go one step further.

Key Principle 2:

The second step out of loneliness is to be honest with yourself and with God, and to seek friendship and emotional support of other people.

Key Verses:

1 John 1:8
Lamentations 3:40

Teacher Note: Here is a list of questions that will help the lonely student to be more honest with himself:

> Do I really want out of my loneliness?
> Do I show my thoughts of isolation by the expression on my face?
> Am I really unnecessarily afraid of people?
> If so, why am I afraid of them?
> Do I really believe God can help solve my loneliness problem?
> Am I willing to be hurt to love others?
> What am I trying to protect by withdrawing? Is it working?
> What are the consequences?
> Do I realize that being a continual loner means being out of God's will?
> Am I being a loner just to get attention? Or feel sorry for myself?

Transparency #29

Supporting Verses:

> Hebrews 10:24,25
> Romans 1:12

Teacher Note: Once the loner is honest with himself, honesty with God is the next important step.

Key Verses:

> 1 Peter 5:7
> Job 16:19-21

Teacher Note: Stress that some people are afraid to be honest with God because He is too big to be bothered by the details of their lives, or they are afraid He will come down on their ways. Reassure your students that God never cut anyone down for being honest with Him. God says to cast all cares on Him in 1 Peter 5:7.

Key Questions:

1. What does casting mean, in 1 Peter 5:7?

2. What are anxieties?

3. What are some anxieties about loneliness we can cast on God?

Supporting Verse:

> James 1:5 *If any lack wisdom*

Project:

Hand out a sheet of paper to each student. Have every student write out a model prayer that they might say to God when they are really lonely.

Key Verses:

Galatians 6:2
Ephesians 4:25

Teacher Note: Your students need to realize that God has designed brothers and sisters in Christ to help them through crisis situations. Also, they do not need to lie or cover-up the way they really feel. Ephesians 4:25 says it is possible to tell or live a lie before brothers and sisters without using words.

Key Questions:

1. From Ephesians 4:25, what are some ways brothers and sisters in Christ can lie to one another?

2. From Galatians 6:2, who gets cheated when others aren't included in our times of need?

Teacher Note: Jesus was the best example of relationships, because in His strongest hour of distress He turned to the Father and His friends. In Matthew 26:36-40 Jesus took His disciples to the garden not only to pray but to comfort Him when He needed support the most.

Wrap Up/Application:

Challenge your students to pray for anyone they may know who is in an emotional tailspin. Also, pray that God will help them to look for people who are lonely, so they may love them and counsel them. Also, they must pray that when they get lonely, God will remind them to have a good talk with themselves.

LONELINESS
Lesson 10
Part 2 of Chapter 4
(pages 71-80)

Introduction/Review:

In the "Loneliness" chapter all of the key principles are tied closely together, therefore, a thorough review is important.

Here are some review questions to ask your students about the last lesson. If your students cannot remember a particular answer, you need to answer for them so that the previous material stays fresh in their minds.

1. What are some of the definitions of loneliness discussed in the last lesson? (see page 63 of the discussion manual)
2. What is the first step out of loneliness? (answer on page 64)
3. What are the symptoms of someone caught in the tailspin of loneliness? (see page 65)
4. What are some statements we can tell our emotions to help us get hold of ourselves? (answers on page 66)
5. What is the second step out of loneliness? (page 67)
6. Why are some Christians afraid to be honest with God?
7. Why are some Christians afraid to be honest with other Christians? (answers on page 66)
8. Is being honest with other Christians a sign of weakness? Why? Why not?

Key Principles:

1. Another important step out of loneliness is to come to love and understand the presence of God in daily living.

2. The next step out of loneliness is to forget selfish interests and reach out in a giving way to others.

3. One way to avoid emotional pain is to interpret the alone times correctly.

Key Principle 1:

Another important step out of loneliness is to come to love and understand the presence of God in daily living.

Teacher Note: Point out to your students that loneliness is not a circumstance but a condition. Just because your students are alone does not mean they are lonel And simply being around people does not cure loneliness. You may want to ask your students if they have been lonely in a crowd, like in the school cafeteria or in the middle of a pep assembly. Stress that Jesus was a great example of how to be alone but not lonely.

Key Verses:

> John 6:15; 8:29

Key Question:

1. What was Christ's secret in being alone but not lonely?
   (Answer: He knew the Father never left Him alone.)

Teacher Note: On page 73 of the discussion manual are a few examples of when your students may find themselves alone. However, the Bible teaches that they should never be lonely because Christ promises He will never leave them. See Matthew 28:20 and Hebrews 13:5. Some Biblical examples of conquering loneliness are David and Jesus on the Cross. King David understood how to make an alone time worthwhile. He wrote Psalm 63:1 after fleeing to the desert because he was chased by his son, Absalom.

Also, no one understands loneliness more than Jesus Christ. His disciples and even His Father left Him alone to die on the cross. (See Matthew 27:46) Therefore, because Christ died on the cross, He made it possible for us never to be lonely again. That's why David wrote Psalm 27:10.

Key Principle 2:

> The next step out of loneliness is to forget selfish interests and reach out in a giving way to others.

Transparency #30

Teacher Note: Loneliness is common with the majority of high school students because they fail to apply this principle to their lives. Your job is to help your students get their eyes off themselves and serve others who need their friendship. On page 75 of the discussion manual is a box entitled, "Another Word for Loneliness." You need to stress what it says about the "I and me" complex.

Key Verses:

> Romans 15:1
> Matthew 20:26-28
> Philippians 2:3,4

Teacher Note: Before you continue, you may want to list the three attitudes of relating to others on an overhead projector or blackboard.

  A. Attitude of responsibility
  B. Attitude of a servant
  C. Attitude of hard work

A. ATTITUDE OF RESPONSIBILITY

Teacher Note: *Stress that getting out of loneliness is not easy and in order to develop more than a superficial relationship with others, your students need an attitude of responsibility. They need to be involved in other people's lives and not be self-centered.*

Key Verse:

Romans 15:1

Key Questions:

1. What is the responsibility of the strong?

2. Do you know someone who may be weaker than you and who needs your help?

3. What are you doing if you ignore this responsibility?

B. ATTITUDE OF A SERVANT

Transparency #31

Key Verses:

Matthew 20:26-28

Project:

Break your class into three small groups (if your class is large, split into groups of five or seven students). Have each group select someone to record the information. Now, have each group list the answers to these two questions:

1. What were the attributes of a servant in Christ's day? (Examples: No rights to time, privacy, name, respect, pride, family, etc. Had to give up all personal rights.)

2. How did Christ reach out to people and when did He reach out? (Examples: Healing, feeding, speaking, miracles, preaching, etc. Touching the leper, the blind, the lame; reached out to Judas who betrayed Him; reached out to Peter when walking on water; consulted the disciples when they were obnoxious.)

Next, have each group list how the attitude of being a servant helps them reach out to others.

C. ATTITUDE OF HARD WORK

Key Verses:

Philippians 2:3,4

Key Questions:

1. What are the two attitudes we cannot have to reach out to others?
   (Answer: Selfishness and empty conceit.)

2. What should be our attitude?
   (Answer: Humility)

Teacher Note: Most students are afraid to reach out to others, therefore, they need to understand that if they are rejected by someone, the person who is rejecting them probably has a deeper need. Assure your students that they should not get offended if this happens, but should remain patient with the person. You should clearly teach the paragraph entitled, "Taking the Pain Out of Someone's Cold Response to Our Friendship" on page 78 of the discussion manual.

Key Principle 3:

One way to avoid emotional pain is to interpret the alone times correctly.

Transparency #32

Key Verse:

Matthew 14:23

Teacher Note: Stress from this principle that there are times we need to be alone, without being surrounded by noise.

Project:

Select a student of your class to help you with this project. With a tape recorder, tape quick excerpts of all the senseless noise on a rock radio station. (The average high school student listens to rock-n-roll radio 30 hours per week!) Be sure to tape a variety of excerpts, like commercials, loud, obnoxious disc-jockeys and contests. Then play the tape back to your class to let them hear for themselves the kind of mind pollution they hear everyday.

Supporting Verses:

Isaiah 30:15b
Psalm 119:23-24
2 Timothy 4:13

Teacher Note: *Stress that a period of time alone can be a good, productive time. Tell them that they are not failures just because they find themselves alone sometimes. Being alone could be one of the better things that could happen to them.*

Three practical things to do when spending time alone:

I. THINK - God wants us to <u>think</u> when we are alone. See Isaiah 30:15b.

Key Question:

   1. What are some things we can think of when we are alone, that can help us when we are back with people?

II. PRAY - God wants us to get to know Him better by spending time alone in prayer. See Mark 1:35.

Key Question:

   1. Did Jesus fail just because He went to a lonely place to pray?

      A. Often, when we are quiet and alone with the Lord, He faithfully meets our needs.

      B. God may allow you to be in times of aloneness so that you will take the time to pray.

III. READ THE BIBLE - Group Bible studies are fine, but God wants us to spend time alone reading and meditating on His Word. See Psalms 119:23,24.

Key Question:

   1. What did King David do to strengthen himself against his enemies?

IV. READ GOOD BOOKS - God wants us to expand our minds by reading. That is why simply filling our alone times by listening to radio or watching television is a mistake. See 2 Timothy 4:13.

Key Question:

   1. When Paul was in prison he could have spent his time just being depressed. How did he spend his time?

Teacher Note: *Ask your students to tell you when was the last time they read a book simply for pleasure. Then ask them, what was the book? At what times did they read it?*

Wrap Up/Application:

As a teacher, you should realize that many of your students are lonely. Even though those who are lonely have not gone through nearly the loneliness you have experienced, their loneliness is something very real to them.

To conclude the studies on loneliness, challenge your students to make a commitment to God to get hold of their emotions and their time, and to help them reach out to others.

You may want to do this at the end of class time in a special prayer session. For some of your students the prayer will be the most meaningful commitment they will make in the entire relationships series.

PARENTS
Lesson 11
Part 1 of Chapter 5
(pages 83-85)

Introduction:

This chapter could be the most important chapter you teach in the entire series on relationships. Thus far, nothing has affected the lives of your students more than the relationship with their parents. And as your students grow through the sensitive time of adolescence, they will encounter many problems and adjustments with their parents. Therefore, you need to approach the topic of parents carefully so as not to take sides in your student's battles at home. Instead, you need to help your students recognize their responsibilities to their parents and to understand their parent's authority under God. In order to create an atmosphere of openness, be sure to encourage plenty of discussion by your students as you proceed through this lesson. Opening Prayer: Challenge your students as you open this lesson to ask God for a whole new perspective on their parents -- God's perspective.

Project A:

Pass out a sheet of paper to each student and have them answer these questions. You may want to list the questions on an overhead projector or blackboard.

1. Do you know why you have hassles with your parents?

2. Are the conflicts with your parents mostly their fault?

3. Are the conflicts with your parents mostly your fault?

Next, have your students write down what they believe is the percentage of intensity beside each answer (the three should add up to 100%).

For example:

1. Yes, I think I know why we don't get along sometimes. It's because we don't communicate with each other. 35%

2. I'd say many of the conflicts are started by them. 50%

3. I know some of the conflicts seem to be my fault, but not many. 15%

   100%

Now, ask your students why their relationship with their parents will affect the way they view each of the following areas:
* themselves
* their date life
* their studies
* their marriage plans
* their relationships with friends
* their career plans
* their walk with God
* their peace of mind

Project B:

This is an essay assignment so give each student a sheet of paper. Allow your students five minutes to write on the following questions:

1. Choose one area of your relationship with your parents that could be improved.

2. Why did you select this area, and why does it need to be improved?

Then have one or two students share with the class what they have written.

Key Principle:

1. The relationships with parents greatly affects the walk with God.

Transparency #33

Teacher Note: You should teach simply and clearly the Bible's teaching on authority and rebellion. Also, point out how authority and rebellion relates to God through parents. See the top of page 84 of the discussion manual, entitled "Something in Common", for this important concept.

Key Questions:

1. What is the kind of pride that God hates?
   (Answer: The kind of pride God hates causes people to think they are so strong, wise and independent that they do not need to obey God's ways. See Proverbs 16:5 and 8:13.)

2. How does pride show itself in rebellion?
   (Answer: Rebellion shows that since the person is so strong, wise and independent he can resist any authority figure who might tell him what to do or how to live.)

Teacher Note: Stress to your students that nothing has so destructively affected our existence as pride and rebellion. Consequently, a bad habit of rebellion against authority figures causes deep conflict in our walk with God.

Key Verses:

Romans 13:1,2

Therefore, when we reject authority, we are really being rebellious and prideful against God Himself. And that is a big mistake!

Key Questions:

1. According to Romans 13:1-2, how closely related is an authority figure to God?

2. From verse 1, is any person in authority?

Teacher Note: In answering these questions, stress that God does not take the authority of others lightly, and if man chooses to reject authority, God says is making a big mistake.

Supporting Verses:

Proverbs 17:11, 15:5

Wrap Up/Conclusion:

To conclude, tell your students that because their relationship with parents has such a great effect on their lives and on their walks with God, the next three lessons are well worth attending Challenge them to return, as these three lessons could radically change their lives for the better.

PARENTS
Lesson 12

Part 2 of Chapter 5
(pages 85-89)

Introduction/Review:

The last lesson was used basically as an introduction to the importance of students getting along with their parents. Review the main thrust which was that getting along with parents means submitting to the authority of God. A prideful and rebellious attitude towards authority can lead to many problems. In this lesson you will be covering practical steps students can begin taking toward peace with their parents.

Teacher Note: As you begin this lesson, establish that no person can solve a problem unless they really want to solve it. Your students should ask themselves, "How bad do I want to solve the problem?"

Project:

"How Bad" project. You may want to type or write out the following scale and question, then make one copy for each student in your class.

1 2 3 4 5 6 7 8 9 10

1-least intense   10-most intense

My desire to improve my relationship with my parents is _____ on the scale above.

In 2 to 4 sentences, describe why you chose the number above.

BECAUSE _____
_____
_____

After the project is completed, you may want to ask the students what numbers they chose and why.

Teacher Note: Make clear to your students that the counsel you are about to give them is not easy to practice, but since it is from God, it works. Stress, however, that the workability of the counsel still depends on how much they really want to improve their relationship with their parents.

Key Principle:

1. In order to have a better relationship with parents, you must decided to be a peacemaker.

Transparency #34

A. Three qualities you must have to become a peacemaker:

    I. You must not let your parent's weaknesses justify your rebellion against them.
    II. You must have a willingness to become vulnerable.
    III. You must be willing to face injustice.

Key Verse:

Matthew 5:9

Teacher Note: Point out that God says they can have happiness, but there are no shortcuts. Unless your students strive for peace in their families, they will not be happy.

    A. THREE QUALITIES YOU MUST HAVE TO BECOME A PEACEMAKER:

        I. You must not let your parent's weaknesses justify your rebellion against them.

Teacher Note: Don't waste time convincing your students their parents <u>do</u> <u>not</u> have faults because they do have certain weaknesses. Rather, emphasize that their parents' faults do not give them reason to be rebellious.

Transparency #35

Project:

"What's Wrong with my Parents!"

Give <u>each</u> student a sheet of paper. Then, divide the class into groups with four students each. Have your students list on their own papers the complaints about parents that each group can compile collectively. Some of the more common complaints are listed on page 86 of the discussion manual. Your students should think of complaints not on this list.

Have each group appoint a captain who will present the list of the complaints of his group to you. After you receive a list from each group, write the complaints on an overhead projector transparency or blackboard.

Now, have each student write over the top of their list of complaints as you also write over the top of your overhead or blackboard list, the following: "God does not want me to use my parent's weaknesses as justification for my rebellion towards them!" At the end of that sentence, write "I Peter 2:18-20" (just the reference).

After completing this project, stress that God wants them to straighten out their own lives before they can help their parents with their problems.

Key Verse:

    Matthew 7:3-5

Supporting Verses:

    1 Peter 2:18-20 (note that this passage is also included under the third quality of a peacemaker. The first and third qualities overlap in these verses, so use them for both qualities.)

Transparency #36

    II.   You must have a willingness to become vulnerable.

Teacher Note: Most students do not understand what vulnerability means -- to put yourself at the mercy of someone's sensitivity and judgment, thereby running a risk of being misunderstood or hurt by them. You may want to share an illustration from your own life when you became vulnerable to another person, like your parents, wife, employer, children, etc. Jesus is the greatest example of vulnerability. He was vulnerable to the world (John 1:10), to the Father (Philippians 2:8), and to the disciples (Mark 14:32-40).

Transparency #37

Teacher Note: Stress that the student who is a peacemaker stays open to his parents even if he keeps getting hurt.

Key Verse:

    1 Corinthians 13:5

Key Questions:

    1. Have your parents ever wronged you?
    2. What was your reaction?
    3. How do you feel about the incident now?
    4. From the key verse, how should we handle wrong?

    III.   You must be willing to face injustice.

Teacher Note: Stress that parents not only made mistakes in the past, but will also make mistakes in the future. Tell them that the secret of being at peace with themselves, God, and others is learning how to face injustices.

Key Verses:

    1 Peter 2:18-20

Key Questions:

1. According to verse 18, should we respect only good and loving authorities?

2. According to verse 20, what should our attitude be when we are wronged?

3. According to verse 20, how does God respond to our patience when we face injustice?

Supporting Verses:

    Matthew 10:34-36

Teacher Note: Point out that students who have non-Christian parents or parents who are carnal (out of fellowship with God) are likely to suffer greater misunderstanding and persecution within their own homes.

Key Question:

1. Why do you think misunderstanding and persecution could happen in a non-Christian or carnal home?

Wrap Up/Conclusion:

    Explain to your students that God does not want them to be surprised when they are treated unjustly. God wants them to look after their parents needs, to be vulnerable to them, and to expect to be treated unfairly. <u>God just wants them to love their parents in His power</u>. If they trust God in these areas of their relationships, they are on their way to happiness.

PARENTS
Lesson 13
Part 3 of Chapter 5
(pages 89-94)

Introduction/Review:

Review the last two lessons on parents by asking some of the key questions from the lesson. Take no more than five or seven minutes for review. Then, prepare your students for what they are going to hear in this lesson. This lesson probably will be the most pointed and convicting lesson on parents so far. You need to assure them that you are not taking sides with their parents, but only giving counsel from God's Word. Let your students know that carrying out this counsel will not be easy, but if they practice it, peace with their parents is guaranteed.

Key Principles:

1. Not only must you be a peacemaker, but you must learn to obey your parents in order to have real happiness in your home.

2. There are seven practical steps you should take to create a better relationship with your parents.
   a. Seek your parents' forgiveness.
   b. Cooperate with your parents.
   c. Tell your parents you love them.
   d. Thank your parents for all they have done for you.
   e. Avoid raising your voice with your parents.
   f. Let God change your parents' mind; that's His job, not yours.
   g. Astound your parents by the over-obedient method.

Key Principle 1:

Not only must you be a peacemaker, but you must learn to obey your parents in order to have real happiness in your home.

Key Verses:

Ephesians 6:1-3

Key Questions:

1. Why should we obey parents?
2. What are the benefits of obeying parents?
3. Why will we live longer if we obey our parents?

Answers: **A.** Some teenagers are killed as direct result of disobeying parents (e.g. overdose of drugs or alcohol, playing with guns, fighting, drunk driving, runaway).

B. *A less conspicuous killer is the psychological effect of anxiety. (e.g. bitterness, resentment, hatred, guilt, fear, worry). When a person does not make peace with his parents he is likely to suffer from many of these anxieties, thereby shortening his life.*

Teacher Note: *Your students need to know that God's counsel is given for a reason, and that God is not trying to make them miserable by obeying their parents.*

Illustration:

There are at least two abilities God has given parents so they can help students grow as people.

A. *Parents have the ability to perceive events, people and circumstances that will harm us.*
B. *Parents have the ability to discern rough edges in our attitudes which could be detrimental to our lives.*

Key Verses:

Proverbs 5:12-14

Supporting Verse:

Proverbs 12:15

Teacher Note: *The basic concepts of parents' abilities are located on pages 90 and 91 of the discussion manual. You should cover these concepts so that your students will begin to better appreciate their parents' worth.*

A. PARENTS HAVE THE ABILITY TO PERCEIVE EVENTS, PEOPLE AND CIRCUMSTANCES THAT WILL HARM US.

Transparency #38

Illustration:

Tell a story of yourself or someone you may know who did not listen to the wise counsel of parents, and as a result, got into trouble. Then ask your students to think about an instance when they ignored their parent's counsel, which ended in harm to them.

Project A:

Pass out a sheet of paper to every fourth student in the class. Now, divide the class into groups of four, with each person who received a sheet of paper as the group leader. Next, have each group list the things they say and do that upset their parents. After each group has compiled a list, have the leaders read their group's list of things as you write them on the overhead projector transparency or on the blackboard.

B. PARENTS HAVE THE ABILITY TO DISCERN ROUGH EDGES IN OUR ATTITUDES WHICH COULD BE DETRIMENTAL

Transparency #39

Project B:

Project A must be completed before starting this project. From the following list of attitudes (also found on pages 91 and 92 of the discussion manual, with the exception of "rebellion"), have each group of four determine which attitude led to the behaviors they listed from Project A.

* *Laziness*
* *Ungratefulness*
* *Temper*
* *Pride*
* *Rudeness*
* *Selfishness*
* *Sloppiness*
* *Unforgiving Spirit*
* *Rebellion*

Teacher Note: *The paragraph on page 92 of the discussion manual under "It is absolutely crucial..." teaches that God uses other people to smooth off the rough edges in students' lives if they do not listen to their parents. You need to emphasize the teaching in this paragraph.*

Supporting Verses:

Proverbs 15:31,32; 3:11,12

Key Principle 2:

There are seven practical steps you should take to contribute to a better relationship with your parents.

Transparency #40

Teacher Note: *You are about to teach some difficult concepts. They are seven practical steps that your students can take to get peace with their parents and God. But first have your students answer the following key questions in their hearts and minds.*

Key Questions:

1. *Have you done something in any way that has hurt your parents?*

2. Are you cooperating with God as He works through your parents to smooth out some of your rough spots?

Teacher Note: Your job is to encourage the students in your group, especially those who might be out of fellowship with their parents, to share these four steps (also listed on page 93 of the discussion manual).

1. Seek your parents' forgiveness.
2. Cooperate with your parents.
3. Tell your parents you love them.
4. Thank your parents for all they have done for you.

Be sure you have studied these first four steps well, so as not to mislead your students in this crucial situation. Also, you need to prepare your students for different kinds of responses they may get from their parents. Some parents may cry, some may get defensive, some may even ask for forgiveness. But, what they need to realize in seeking their parent's forgiveness, is that they are doing what God wants, and that He will greatly reward them for obeying Him.

Supporting Verses:

Matthew 5:23,24

Teacher Note: Steps five, six and seven are self-explanatory in the discussion manual.

5. Avoid raising your voice with your parents.
6. Let God change your parent's mind; that's His job, not yours.
7. Astound your parents by the over-obedient method.

Wrap Up/Conclusion:

Some of the students in your class may have come to the deciding point in terms of making peace with their parents. As you conclude by praying aloud, challenge each student that if the Holy Spirit has been speaking to him, he needs to make peace with his family by applying steps one through four.

Word of Caution. This is one of the hardest decisions a high school student could make in his/her young life. Therefore, you must make this challenge with much sensitivity and after much prayer.

PARENTS
Lesson 14
Part 4 of Chapter 5
(pages 94-96)

Introduction:

Before you begin this last lesson on parents, review the previous key principles of the last three lessons with your students. Also, ask if any of the students shared the first four steps of the last lesson with their parents. If so, ask if they would like to share with the class the experience and the results since that time. In this lesson, you as the teacher, will be encouraging your students to look at life and problems from their parents' perspective. You will be encouraging them to be selfless and compassionate, as well as giving, to their parents. Like the other lessons, this lesson will not be an easy task, because as you know, some high school students tend to be selfish and self-centered.

Key Principle:

1. One step towards having a happy home is to see life from your parents' point of view.

Project:

In this exercise, get your students to list the answers to these two important questions:

1. What are the good qualities of my parents?
2. What are some of the needs of my parents?

To start, pass out a sheet of paper, blank on both sides, to each student. They will be writing on both sides. At the very top middle have the students write "Father" on one side of the paper and "Mother" on the other side. Have the students draw a line down the middle (top to bottom) on both sides. On both sides, at the top left hand side have them write, "What are the good qualities of my father/mother?" Now, have the students list the things that come to mind under each category. After they have finished, ask your student to share some of the things they have listed as you copy good examples on an overhead projector or blackboard in the same manner.

Key Verse:

Philippians 2:3,4

Key Question:

1. How does the instruction of this verse relate to the way you treat your parents?

Teacher Note: Stress to your students that God calls them to actively love and serve their parents. And God expects high school students to bring great joy to their parents. Refer to Proverbs 10:1. Assure them that they can bring great joy by being compassionate and understanding of their father and mother.

THE NEEDS AND EMOTIONAL PRESSURES OF DAD

Key Question:

1. What are some of the emotional pressures your father is facing that cause him to act the way he does?
   (Answer: On page 94 of the discussion manual is a sample list. Encourage your students to verbalize their own answers and what they mean.)

Teacher Note: After the students share some of their answers, point out that the last thing their father needs is for them to be rebellious and insensitive to him, especially if he has real hurts.

Supporting Verse:

Proverbs 25:20

THE NEEDS AND EMOTIONAL PRESSURES OF MOM

Transparency #41

Teacher Note: Now have your students discuss with you some of the needs and emotional pressures of their mother. On the top of page 95 is an example list of some of the problems mothers experience. Refer to this list only when your students cannot think of more; encourage them to verbalize their own examples.

Project:

Divide your class into groups with no more than five in a group. No writing is necessary, just open discussion. Have each group think of things that high school students can do for their parents and activities they can do with their parents. Tell them these are the kinds of actions that demonstrate how much students love their parents.

Supporting Verse:

1 John 3:18

Teacher Note: *On page 95 of the discussion manual is a list of activities students can do for both father and mother. Please add any of your own suggestions to the list, if possible. Encourage your students to try some of these activities at the next opportunity.*

Wrap Up/Application:

Your students have heard and discussed much about their parents in the last four lessons. An appropriate conclusion to this series on parents would be a challenge to your students, especially those having parental problems, to pray for the needs of their parents. Encourage them, also, to pray that God will show them activities they can do with their parents in order that the relationship might grow.

SEX
Lesson 15
Part 1 of Chapter 6
(page 99-103)

Teacher Note: *The next two lessons on sex may be somewhat embarrassing or uncomfortable for you to teach. But teaching the topic of sex does not have to be difficult. As you may have noticed already, teenagers are very open to and sometimes blunt in the area of sex. However, most students appreciate an open, honest and clean approach to the subject of sex. Your students will not be embarrassed if you are not embarrassed. Remember, the world's view of sex is constantly bombarding students. They desperately need to know God's perspective on sex. What you share with students on God's perspective could save them hours of pain, guilt and worry.*

The authors of the Teacher's Guide have designed the chapter in the discussion manual on sex into two lessons only. Don't thwart discussion on this subject just to cover all of the material provided. Each lesson may take twice as long to teach as intended by the authors. Whatever rate you choose to complete these two lessons, be sure you thoroughly cover at least the key principles.

Transparency #42

Introduction:

Basically, you need to get your students verbalizing on the subject of sex in order to know where they stand.
Here are some good questions to kick off the discussion on sex:

1. Do you believe that sex is "dirty?"
2. Should sex be used only for the purpose of producing children?
3. Do you think sex before marriage is justifiable because:

   * it helps you understand your true feelings about the other person?
   * you plan on marriage soon anyway?
   * it will teach you how to be a better lover in marriage?
   * this intimate method will help you know if you're compatible?

4. Do you think sex before marriage is wrong? Why?
5. How far sexually should you go with your date? (Teacher, don't spend too much time on this question; it's a rhetorical question.)

Key Principles:

1. Sex has a great influence on your life because of three things:

   * sex drives
   * emotional and security drives
   * a sex crazed society

2. God views sex as a good thing, and He has approved of the sex relationship between a husband and his wife.

Key Principle 1:

Sex has a great influence on your life because of three things.

   A.   SEX DRIVES

Teacher Note: *No doubt, many of your students think they are the only ones who ever had sex drives and needs. You need to point out (as explained on page 100 of the discussion manual) that a sex drive, in and of itself, is not sin. After all, God understands strong sex impulses because He creatively designed them. Nevertheless, having a strong physical drive is one of the key reasons why students are involved with sex today.*

Supporting Verse:

    1 Corinthians 7:9

   B.   EMOTIONAL AND SECURITY DRIVES

Teacher Note: *A strong tie exists between a student's emotional drives (to be loved, to love and to be secure) and his/her heavy sexual involvement (as discussed on page 101 of the discussion manual). You need to stress, however, that if a student's emotional needs get out of control, they can lead to heavy sexual involvement which invariably leads to many negative consequences. That is why God counsels us to exercise self-control with our emotions.*

Supporting Verse:

    Proverbs 4:23

   C.   OUR SOCIETY IS SEX CRAZY

Transparency #43

Project:

    Gather together at least three of each of the following and present them to your class.

       * rock songs that have sexual overtones
       * magazine advertisements with sexual connotations
       * examples of television programs that emphasize sex

After this project, your students will begin to realize how much this society uses sex to sell and entertain.

Transition:

Since we have such strong physical and emotional drives and live in a sex crazy society, many students are confused about the right and wrong uses of sex. Therefore, we need to discuss what God says about sex.

Key Principle 2:

God views sex as a good thing, and He has approved of the sexual relationship between a husband and his wife.

A.   GOD IS FOR SEX

Teacher Note: Some students have the idea that God simply tolerates sex and that Christians are down on sex. Your job is to dispel that idea in a real and honest way. Assure your students that God is pro sex because He created sex and designed the human sexual equipment.

Key Verse:

Genesis 1:27,28,31

Key Questions:

1. Is it possible to be fruitful and multiply and fill the earth without sex?
2. What was God's attitude when He designed sex?

Illustration:

God could have created babies in many other ways other than by sexual intercourse. He could have dropped them from the sky, or delivered them via the stork, or planted them under rocks. But God didn't do it that way. He thought the best way to be fruitful and multiply was through a sexual relationship.

B.   JESUS CHRIST APPROVED OF SEX BETWEEN A HUSBAND AND HIS WIFE.

Supporting Verse:

Matthew 19:4-6

Key Question:

1. What did Jesus mean by, "the two shall become one flesh"?

(Answer: Becoming one flesh means two people coming together in the most intimate act possible, through sexual relations.)

Transition:

God created sex not only for reproducing babies and for sealing marriage vows through the act of becoming one flesh, but He also designed sex to be pleasurable for the ones involved.

Key Verse:

Proverbs 5:18,19

Key Questions:

1. What did Solomon mean by, "rejoice in the wife of your youth?"

Supporting Verse:

1 Corinthians 7:2-5 (Living Bible) (Teacher read this passage to the class and ask them what it says about marriage and sex. The Living Bible clarifies this passage in terms students can better understand.)

Wrap Up/Conclusion:

You need to stress to your students that the series on sex will continue in the next lesson, which discusses God's view on sex before marriage. Repeat to your students that God is pro sex and that He wants most people to enjoy sex to the fullest. But also tell them that a big problem with most high school students is that they are having sex more and enjoying it less.

In your closing prayer you might thank God for creating sex and for designing the joy of sex. Perhaps this lesson and closing prayer will help your students to begin recognizing God's perspective on sex. See James 1:17 for a good supporting reference.

SEX
Lesson 16
Part 2 of Chapter 6
(pages 103-107)

Introduction:

In order to present the material in this lesson, a thorough review of the last lesson on sex must happen. As you review that God is pro sex at the proper time and wants all people to be fulfilled sexually, also stress that God always has good reasons for His loving commands.

Key Questions:

1. Why does God say do not lie?
2. Why does God say do not steal?
3. Why does God say do not murder?

(Answer: God commands certain things for obvious reasons. God has good reasons for giving His commands in the area of sex, too.)

Key Principles:

1. God clearly favors sex within marriage, but He flatly opposes sex or heavy petting before marriage.
2. God wants us to seek and experience the meaning of love.

Key Principle 1:

God clearly favors sex within marriage, but He flatly opposes sex or heavy petting before marriage.

Key Verses:

1 Thessalonians 4:3-5

Key Questions:

1. According to the key verses, what is God's will as we face sexual sin?
2. What is sexual sin?
3. What condition does God want us to be in when we marry?
4. What will happen if we do not stay clear of sexual sin?

Teacher Note: The words "sexual sin" in the Living Bible, or "sexual immorality" in the <u>New American Standard Bible</u> can be defined as fornication, which means sex between two single people. Adultery, on the other hand, means sex with someone other than the marriage partner.

Supporting Verses:

Ephesians 5:3,4

Key Questions:

1. According to the supporting verses, does God tolerate any degree of sexual sin?
2. What are the other activities related to the misuse of sex?

Project:

Proverbs 5 is a chapter in which Solomon speaks to his young son about sexual sin. As graphic and painful as it may seem, have one of your students read this chapter aloud before the class. After the student has finished reading, ask the entire class these discussion questions:

* Can you see some negative consequences from rowdy sexual living?
* What are they?

Teacher Note: For more references speaking directly to the subject of fornication see I Corinthians 6:18; 7:2; 10:8 and Colossians 3:5

Transparency #44

Transition:

God says "no" to premarital sex because He loves us, not because He is the great "killjoy" on sex. God gives us His wise counsel so that we will be able to enjoy sex more not less. Let's study some reasons why God has given us commands on sex.

Key Principle 2:

God wants us to seek and experience the <u>true</u> meaning of love.

Key Verses:

Matthew 22:37-40

Key Question:

1. From Matthew 22:37-40 God gives us the two most important aspects of having a fulfilled, true life. Does God mention sex in the passage?

Transparency #45

Teacher Note: Stress to your high school students that sex has been overrated by man, while God says that love is the most important thing in life.

Supporting Verses:

1 Corinthians 13:1-3

Teacher Note: In order to illustrate the two boxes entitled "What Sex Is Not" and "What Sex Is" on pages 105 and 106 of the discussion manual, here is a line of reasoning you may want to write on an overhead projector or a blackboard:

* Love is not sex.
* Sex is not love.
* Sex is designed to be an expression of love.
* Sex for sex's sake cannot produce love.
* Sex cannot produce love, but sex can stir up desires to be loved.

Therefore, sex for sex's sake cannot meet the need of one who wants to be loved, but only makes the desire for sex more intense. After presenting this statement to your students, explain that <u>sex is not a short cut</u> to finding love.

Transparency #46

Project:

The chart entitled "love" and "Sex-for-Sex's-Sake" (pages 106 and 107 of the discussion manual) lists the differences between true love and sex. Many students are confused about what the differences are and why. Slowly read to your class the items on this chart, carefully comparing each statement on the left with the corresponding statement on the right. Have the students follow along in their manuals as you read.

Teacher Note: The chart should point to an obvious fact about your students' date life, that a heavy sexual dating relationship will self-destruct. At this time show transparencies # 47 and 48. (If you do not have these transparencies use the following illustration. Or for best results, use both these transparencies and the illustration.)

Transparency #47
Transparency #48

Illustration:

Picture in your mind a man who is very, very hungry. After several days of not eating, he buys a hot fudge sundae and eats it. A few hours pass, and he begins to get hungry again. So he devours a piece of chocolate cream pie. The next day the man wakes up feeling a little sick, so he figures he's just hungry and buys a dozen donuts. Quickly he eats all twelve donuts. This sort of eating goes on for a couple of days, and soon the man gets very sick. For over ten days the man has not eaten any nutritious food.

A dating relationship can be the same way as the sick man. The main ingredients that feed a healthy relationship are trust, respect, open communication, honest spiritual communication and deep friendship. These five qualities can be considered the main course of a dating relationship. God has designed sex to be the dessert for married people.

You see, in order to be full and to be healthy in your dating relationship, God wants you to feast on just the main course, which is really all you need. Sex is not necessary for a good, healthy dating relationship, just as dessert is not necessary for a healthy body. While sex in a marriage relationship is an important expression of love, sex in a dating relationship serves no healthy purpose.

Wrap Up/Conclusion:

Close this lesson in prayer by challenging each student to thank God for true love, and for sex that fulfills love in marriage. Also, challenge each student to pray that he will have the glue-like qualities that lead to a healthy dating relationship.

SEX
Lesson 17
Part 3 of Chapter 6
(pages 107-113)

Introduction:

In the last lesson some heavy concepts were covered that your class has probably given little thought to since. You may want to review the last lesson by asking, "What is the difference between love and sex for sex's sake?" and "How come a dating relationship involved in heavy sexual activity almost always ends in destruction?"

As you teach this lesson, stress again that God loves us by giving us commands on sex. Also, be sure to tell your students that God is a forgiving God, because you will probably stir up a lot of guilt in some of your students.

Key Principles:

1. God gives commands concerning sex to protect us from harmful psychological and physical effects.
2. God gives commands concerning sex to protect our future marriage.
3. God gives commands concerning sex to preserve our dignity.

Key Principle 1:

God gives commands concerning sex to protect our future marriages.

Key Verses:

Proverbs 4:15-20

Teacher Note: Stress now that sex is not simply a physical activity. Explain that it is also a psychological event which effects us for good and for bad emotionally. Sex is such a powerful explosive event that it can cause either tremendous good or bad depending on how it is used.

Illustration:

To best illustrate the explosive potential of sex (good or bad) you may want to bring a handful of dirt into your class, although the dirt is not necessary for this illustration.

A door-to-door salesman knocked on the front door of a very big and plush house. He was selling growing soil. The housewife answered the door and invited the salesman in, at which point he began his sales pitch and drew a handful of rich, black soil from his bag. He said, "This soil is the best soil available for growing plants, fruit and vegetables. An acre of this soil sells for thousands of dollars." Then, all of a sudden, the salesman threw the handful of soil onto the woman's plush shag carpet. The woman screamed at the man and yelled, "Clean up that dirt and get out of my house now!" at this point, the rich, black Soil---some of the best growing and most expensive soil available---became nothing more than dirt.

So too, sex when practiced at the wrong time, out of the context of marriage becomes just like dirt.

Teacher Note: Stress these three harmful effects of the misuse of sex:

1. Unfulfilled emotional needs that lead to frustration and bitterness.
2. The potential of developing a crippling emotional habit.
3. The disappointment and boredom in trying to find pleasure. (On page 109 of the discussion manual these three psychological effects are extensively explained. Since this chart provides a lot of material, you may wish to ask these pertinent questions.)

QUESTIONS FOR THE FIRST PSYCHOLOGICAL EFFECT:

1. Why do people involved in premarital sex come away from their experience bitter?
2. What does a person mean who says, "I feel used," after having sex?
3. Why do some students become more emotionally dependent on their partner after having sex with them?

QUESTIONS FOR THE SECOND PSYCHOLOGICAL EFFECT:

1. Why do students get "hooked" on sex?
2. What are some hang-ups for people who have sex for sex's sake?
3. Why doesn't the person who bed-hops ever find the perfect sexual experience?

(Answer: A good sex act is not simply a good physical act. It is a perfect emotional act found only in live by marriage. A bed-hopper is like a man trying to find apples in a peachtree.)

4. How can a person hung-up on sex have a ravaged mind?

QUESTIONS FOR THE THIRD PSYCHOLOGICAL EFFECT:

1. Why are many students disappointed when they have sex out of wedlock?
2. Why are some students bored with sex?

Transition:

Not only can the misuse of sex have harmful psychological effects, but when used improperly sex can also have a bad effect on marriage.

Key Principle 2:

God gives commands concerning sex to protect our future marriages.

Key Verses:

Matthew 19:4-9

Key Questions:

1. What is the degree of solidarity we should have in a marriage relationship?
2. What are the only grounds for divorce?

Teacher Note: Tell your class that statistics show half of all marriage counseling deals with adultery. And half of all the people who are counseled on adultery eventually get a divorce.

Example: Satan vs. Jesus Christ in Matthew 4:14

Transition:

Getting married will not necessarily solve problems of lust or self-control that we have when we are single. At the bottom of page 110 and top of page 111 of your discussion manual are five reasons why a lack of self-control in dating will have harmful effects after marrying. Let's discuss these reasons.

Supporting Verses:

Proverbs 25:28
Galatians 5:22,23

Key Principle 3:

God gives commands concerning sex to preserve our dignity.

Transparency #49

Teacher Note: Point out to your students that our bodies are more than just glands, skin and bones. Our bodies are made in the image of God with a sense of mobility, worthiness and honor. In short, our bodies are valuable. Our bodies are interwoven with our souls and self worth. Satan's goal is to strip away our dignity and to convince us that we are worth nothing. One way he accomplishes this is by luring us into burning physical passions.

Illustration:

When Jesus was tempted in the wilderness, Satan attacked His lower needs, which included food, air, water, rest, etc. When these needs are not satisfied, they become very strong drives. Sex is not a lower need; therefore, it is not a strong drive like food and water. After fasting 40 days, Jesus was tempted with food by Satan. Jesus Christ told Satan that He was trusting God's Word to provide the food He needed.

Satan will come to you saying, "Hey, your passions are the most important of all things. You had better get all the kicks you can to satisfy these desires while you still have them." Your answer to Satan is, "I will trust God, for He will provide for all my needs." You are worth more than what your glands dictate.

You are a person with honor, self-worth and the ability to love. God wants you to live in honor.

Supporting Verses:

1 Corinthians 6:18-20

Key Questions:

1. *Why does God put such a high value on our bodies?*
2. *What does the Bible mean by, "Sin against your own body?"*

(Answer: To rob our body's dignity by using it as a plaything or by using someone else's.)

Teacher Note: *Point out that* <u>bitterness</u> *is a result of a ripped up dignity.*

Wrap Up/Application:

Challenge your students to pray that they will give their bodies and sex lives to God. Also that they will pray for God's help to have self-control and dignity in their dating relationships.

For more discussion questions on sex see pages 113-115 in the discussion manual.

DATING
Lesson 18
Part 1 of Chapter 7
(pages 119-126)

Introduction:

The following three lessons on dating will greatly interest your students. Surveys show that high school students think most about how to get members of the opposite sex interested in them.

However, the Bible does not give specific references to the area of dating. Nowhere does the Bible say, "And Joseph met Mary with his camel at the corner of Bagel and Kibutz streets, and they had a date." The point is that in Bible times there was very little dating. But Scripture does give modern man insights for successful relationships and guidelines for marriage. This series on dating will discuss God's goals for students in dating and the qualities to look for in the persons they want to date.

Transparency #50

Opening Discussion Questions:

The following questions will stimulate your students to think about the Lord's role in their date life.

1. Is God in control of your dating relationships?
2. Do you seek God's guidance before asking for or accepting a date?
3. Do you pray before a date that God will have His will that night?
4. If God is in charge of your date life, how do you know?
5. If God is not in control, what element is missing in your dating so that you are not fulfilled?
6. How would it change your relationship if God was in control?
7. Are spiritual matters ever discussed while you are dating?

Key Principles:

1. God's first goal is for us to give Him our date life and future marriage plans.
2. God wants us to have the proper reasons and motives in dating.
3. Because of His love for us, God instructs true Christians not to date unbelievers (people who do not have a personal relationship with Jesus Christ).

Key Principle 1:

God's first goal is for us to give Him our date life and future marriage plans.

Teacher Note: Point out to your students that God is directly involved with the success or failure of their date life. However, this is difficult for Christian students to understand and put into practice.

Key Verse:

    Matthew 6:33

Supporting Verses:

    Psalm 73:25-26
    Job 23:14
    Psalm 84:11

Transparency #51

Teacher Note: Stress that dating is important and God is for dating. However, point out that many students build dating into a god, thereby making a boyfriend or girlfriend more important than having a meaningful relationship with Jesus. Therfore, tell your students that their first goal in life is not to seek a good date life or marriage.

Key Questions:

1. What does Matthew 6:33 <u>not</u> say?

   (Answer: It does not say, "Seek ye first a good date life and marriage and all these things shall be added unto you.")

2. How does the phrase, "all these things shall be added unto you," apply to your dating?

Illustration:

At this point, give an illustration from your own life how your wife or someone you have dated has failed you. Then ask your students to give you answers to this question:

    What are the disadvantages of making your boyfriend/girlfriend as important as Jesus Christ?

    Answers:
    1. You will get out of fellowship with God.
    2. A boyfriend or girlfriend will not give you spiritual power.
    3. Your deepest needs will not be met.
    4. A boyfriend/girlfriend could be gone tomorrow.
    5. A boyfriend/girlfriend will disappoint and fail you.

Transition:

God wants us to be in love with Him so much, that our love for a boyfriend/girlfriend is a distant second. God wants us to be able to say with the Psalmists, "Whom have I in heaven but You? and I desire no one on earth as much as You! My heart fails, my spirits droop, yet God remains! He is the strength of my heart, He is mine forever!" Psalm 73:25-26

Teacher Note: As you probably know, some students in your group (especially the girls) are already anxious about who they will marry. You need to help them realize that they will always have this anxiety until they give their plans to God. And giving their plans to God means that they are willing to go without dating and willing to be single all their life if it is God's will. Remind them that God loves them, and He knows what the best plan is for their lives.

Supporting Verses:

    Job 23:14
    Psalm 84:11

(Quote these verses and write them on an overhead projector or blackboard.)

Key Principle 2:

God wants us to have the proper reasons and motives in dating.

Teacher Note: God encourages students to date for three reasons. Before discussing these reasons, stress that just because a person is not dating does not mean he/she is out of God's will.

Reasons for Dating:

   1. Dating helps us to grow as individuals.

Transparency #52

Key Verses:

    Mark 12:30,31 (Explanation: God uses other people in our lives to influence
                   us.)

Teacher Note: Be sure you can teach the paragraph on page 122 entitled, "In dating, two people come together to share....." The paragraph discusses the importance of adding to our lives the perspective of the opposite sex.

Supporting Verse:

    Proverbs 27:17

Project:

This project may make some of your students too sensitive to the areas discussed, so prepare and execute with caution.

To begin with, ask your students to raise their hands if they have already dated. From those who raised their hands, select three or four students to come to the front for a panel/audience discussion. Have each student on the panel, one by one, <u>share what their dating experience taught them about themselves</u>. Encourage the student audience and other panel members to ask questions and discuss their answers.

    2. Dating allows us to contribute to the growth of another person.

Key Verse:

Romans 14:19

Teacher Note: As you probably know, high school students tend to have the "either/or syndrome." Meaning, <u>either</u> a person is a potential boyfriend/girlfriend, <u>or</u> they are not. Therefore, stress that girls ought to have guys as just friends, and vise versa. Explain that non-romantic friends can encourage one another to grow as well as boyfriends or girlfriends.

Illustration:

Again, draw from your own personal experience of how someone of the opposite sex who you were not involved with romantically helped you to grow.

    3. Dating helps us to get prepared for the right marriage partner.

Key Verse:

Jeremiah 12:5

Teacher Note: Point out to your students that dating can be used for just good, clean fun. But, in the minds of students who are dating, they are looking for the special someone who will eventually become their marriage partner.

    a. Dating can show us the personalities we are most compatible with.
    b. Dating can teach us to be sensitive to other people.
    c. Dating can reveal areas in our lives that we need to straighten out before marriage.

(For a more extensive explanation of these last three areas see page 123 of the discussion manual.)

Key Principle 3:

Because of His love for us, God instructs true Christians not to date unbelievers.

Teacher Note: You are about to discuss one of the most delicate and explosive areas in the personal lives of your students. The girls, particularly, struggle with this instruction, so be firm but gentle as you discuss it. Girls are *frustrated because they want to do God's will, but are socially pressured to date. Plus, there are few Christian guys to date, and those Christian guys who are available will not ask them out on a date.*

How your students cope with this instruction could have a greater influence on their walk with God, while they are in high school and college, than any other issue they face. God's Word is clear on the subject of dating non-Christians. Therefore, how your students deal with this instruction comes to the point of whether they will "receive in humility" (James 1:21) His counsel or reject it.

Key Verses:

2 Corinthians 6:14,15

Key Questions:

1. *When you spend time dating a person, do you become somewhat like a team with him?*
2. *If you are dating a non-Christian, what things do you have in common?*
3. *What things do you not have in common?*

Supporting Verses:

Titus 3:3
Ephesians 4:17,18
Psalm 1:1

Teacher Note: *Stress that we begin thinking like the people we spend time with; therefore, whoever we date has a tremendous spiritual and emotional effect on us. Share this statement with your students;*

God knows that an unbeliever will not help us to focus our attention on Him or His ways.

Transition:

God is positive about who we should spend our time with, especially during our youth years. Let's read 2 Timothy 2:22 together.

POPULAR QUESTION ASKED BY STUDENTS:

"Should I still date a non-Christian even with the intention of leading them to Jesus Christ?"

Answers for Girls:

1. Generally, guys are too proud to listen.
2. Guys are more interested in the girl than in her message.
3. If the guy is interested in knowing about spiritual matters, the girl should direct him to another Christian guy for spiritual counsel.

Answers for Guys:

> *Guys have no excuse for dating non-Christian girls, because there are many fine Christian girls to date. If a guy wants to lead a girl to Christ, he can do so without dating.*

Teacher Note: *A full discussion on the differences between Christian and non-Christian students is on pages 125 and 126 of the discussion manual.*

Wrap Up/Conclusion:

Challenge your students to pray for:

1. *Thank God for the privilege of dating.*
2. *Ask Him to take control of your date life.*
3. *Tell Him you want to grow and help others grow through dating.*
4. *Ask for power to say no to the non-Christian and power to say yes to Christian dates.*

DATING
Lesson 19
Part 2 of Chapter 7
(pages 127-132)

Introduction:

This lesson deals with the qualities that make up the kind of man women seek. Even though the lesson is about the girls, the guys in your class will learn what qualities women look for and how women think.

Project:

Hand out a sheet of paper to every student. Have the girls complete this sentence on their papers:

"When I think of the perfect guy to date, I would describe his qualities as (name six) .

Have the guys complete this sentence:

"When girls look for the perfect guy to date, I think they look for qualities like (name six) .

After the students have written out their six answers, select four girls to sit on a discussion panel in front of the class. Now, have each of the four girls on the panel describe the six qualities she wrote down. As they tell you the qualities list them on an overhead projector or blackboard. Ask the guys in your class to listen and compare the six qualities they listed as the discussion panel proceeds. Interview girls on the panel individually, asking them what each quality means to them and have them give specific examples of when they have seen it practiced.

Key Principle:

1. God's counsel shares with girls the qualities their dates should possess.

Transparency #53

Key Verse:

Psalm 27:4

A. He should be a man who seeks after God.

Key Question:

1. Does your date match up with God's standards as a man to date?

(Answer: One way to know if a guy seeks God is by his speech. Jesus taught that what is inside a man's heart will eventually show up in his speech. See Mark 7:20-23.)

Rhetorical Questions for Girls:

1. Does your boyfriend talk about everything but spiritual matters?
2. How much does your boyfriend speak of spiritual issues?
3. Does your boyfriend express how God will fit into your future plans?
4. Does he continually talk down other Christians?

Teacher Note: Stress to your girls that guys who say they will discuss spiritual matters after they get to know you better, should be watched closely. If a guy does not take the initiative in spiritual things at the beginning of your relaationship, he certainly will not do it after he has won your confidence.

All in all, stress to your girls that finding a man who knows Christ is vitally important. But what's more important is that he wants to develop the quality of seeking God first in his life. Assure your girls that if they settle for anyone who falls short of this goal, they will become frustrated and unfulfilled. If their deepest desire is to seek God with all of their heart, then the man they marry should be more of a seeker.

B. He should be a leader in the relationship.

Supporting Verses:

Ephesians 5:22,23 (Explanation: The personal qualities developed during dating will contribute to marriage. Therefore, a man should begin leading in a dating situation so as to be prepared.)

Luke 22:25-27

Transparency #54

Teacher Note: Point out that regardless of the popular thought of today, God has designed roles for men and women. One of the functions He has designed for men is leadership. And a true leader is nothing more than a servant.

Illustration:

Jesus Christ is the greatest example of a true leader. He served man through word, miracles, healing, salvation, etc. Yet, He was never self-centered. He never bullied anyone around.

QUESTIONS FOR GIRLS:

1. Does your boyfriend order you to do things without asking meaningful questions?
2. Does your boyfriend truly listen to your answers to meaningful questions?

3. Does he make demands and then insinuate you are worthless when you disagree?
4. Does he respect your point of view?
5. Does he kindly let you know how he feels?
6. Does he ask your opinion when making a decision concerning your responsibility.

Transparency #55

Teacher Note: Tell your girls that some guys try to get out of the responsibility for sexual control. (See page 129 in discussion manual.) Then stress that if he states he has little self-control he is "copping out" on his leadership responsibility.

Supporting Verse:

1 Timothy 5:2

C. He should have an attitude of humility with thoughtfulness.

Key Verse:

1 Peter 3:7

Supporting Verse:

Proverbs 15:33

Teacher Note: Point out to the girls that one of the biggest weaknesses of young men is that they are proud. In their desire to be masculine, they fail to realize that true masculinity is characterized by humility and thoughtfulness.

Key Questions:

1. What should the man of God be thoughtful of in dealing with a woman?
2. According to 1 Peter 3:7, what happens to a man who does not treat his wife with thoughtfulness and honor?

Teacher Note: Listed on pages 130 and 131 of the discussion manual are several characteristics of a thoughtful man. The following rhetorical questions concern these characteristics. Direct them at your girls.

The Characteristics of Sensitivity:

1. In what ways does a woman respond emotionally to a man?
2. Why should a man clarify misconceptions as to what he says, as opposed to what a woman thinks he said?

The Characteristics of Humility:

1. How do you feel when a guy asks you for forgiveness?
2. How do you feel towards a guy who admits weakness or fear?

The Characteristic of Encouragement:

1. What are some hobbies or interests of yours that would interest him?

The Characteristics of Praise:

1. What are some positive qualities of yours that a guy could praise?
2. How do you feel when you are praised?

The Characteristics of Honor:

1. How can a guy give honor to you? Others?
2. Why give honor to others who deserve it?

The Characteristics of Patience:

1. In what ways could a woman make a guy impatient?
2. How should a guy respond when he is wronged unnecessarily?

The Characteristics of Provider:

1. If your date refused to pay on dates or get a job to provide for himself, how would you feel?
2. What should you do with a guy who refuses to work or pay bills?

Wrap Up/Conclusion:

Challenge your girls to pray that God will bring a man into their life who seeks after God, who is a leader, and who is humble and thoughtful.

Challenge your guys to pray that God will work to build these important characteristics into their lives, so that they will be properly equipped to love the right woman.

DATING
Lesson 20
Part 3 of Chapter 7
(pages 133-136)

Introduction:

This lesson will be discussing qualities that a guy should seek in a girl as he dates. As the lesson progresses, you need to encourage the guys in your class to verbalize their feelings about dating and women. Generally, expressing deep feelings is difficult for high school guys. Therefore, you need to enter this task prayerfully. Furthermore, your girls will learn a lot from this lesson. They will discover that a substantial amount of ignorance exists between the sexes about the desires of each other. The beginning project is the same project as found in the previous lesson, but applied to the guys of your group.

Project:

Pass out a sheet of paper to each student. Have the guys in your class complete this sentence:

"When I think of the perfect girl to date, I would describe her qualities as ___(name six)___."

Have the girls complete this sentence:

"When guys look for the perfect girl to date, I think they look for qualities like ___(name six)___."

Now, select four guys in the group to form a discussion panel in front of the class. To begin with, have each of the four guys describe each of the qualities he listed as you copy these on an overhead projector or blackboard. While the panel discussion occurs, ask the girls to listen and compare the qualities they listed.

After each guy has read the qualities he listed, interview each one individually Ask them what each quality means and ask them to give specific examples of when they have seen the quality practiced.

Key Principle:

1. God's counsel shares with guys the kind of qualities their dating partner should possess.

Transparency #56

Key Question:

Is she a woman who seeks after God?

Teacher Note: *You need to point out the obvious to your class--most guys get hung-up on the physical attractiveness of a girl. Stress that a guy should be physically attracted to the girl he dates, but he should beware of this point. A beautiful woman may be packaged nicely, but she may lack the qualities contributing to her being a successful date and marriage partner.*

Project:

Give each student a sheet of paper. Have them write, in their own words, what they think Proverbs 11:22 means. You may want to write the verse on an overhead projector or blackboard. Next, ask them to explain their reactions to the idea of "a fine gold ring in a pig's snout."

Here are two sample answers:

> *"What a shame that something as beautiful as a gold ring is covered with pig's snot." "The pig makes the ring look very unattractive."*

Now, ask the class to contrast Proverbs 11:22 with Proverbs 31:30 (you may want to write this verse before them, too.) and explain why the woman in Proverbs 31:30 becomes more attractive.

At this time, tell your class that some guys look for other qualities like good cooking, neatness, sewing, cleanliness, and creativity. While God says these are commendable qualities, they are not the most important.

Supporting Verses:

Luke 10:38-42

Key Question:

1. Even though Martha was a women with many qualities, why would spending more time with Mary be better?

Teacher Note: *The paragraph at the top of page 133 of the discussion manual is worth studying and explaining to your class. After explaining this paragraph in detail to your students, ask the guys these two questions:*

> *"What woman has influenced your life the most for God?"*
> *"What qualities does she have that influence your life the most for God?"*

Supporting Verse:

Proverbs 31:10

Key Question:

1. According to this verse, why does God say that a truly good woman is worth more than precious gems?
2. Is she a woman with a quiet and gentle spirit?

Key Verse:

  1 Peter 3:3,4

Teacher Note: Teach your students what is a quiet and gentle spirit. These short definitions will help you.

  A gentle spirit seeks tenderness and understanding.
  A quiet spirit is not easily anxious or uptight.

Point out that every guy, deep in his own heart, is looking for a gentle and understanding girl. No guy wants a girl who is loud, obnoxious or over sensitive (cries a lot). These qualities are caused by self-centeredness. And a guy especially does not want to marry a contentious woman.

  Emphasize this point by asking the guys in your group these questions:

  1. When your girlfriend is around you, does she complain?
  2. Does she argue at home?
  3. Does she get upset easily when circumstances don't go her way?
  4. Does she belittle (criticize) you in front of others?

Supporting Verse:

  Proverbs 21:19

Key Question:

  1. Why does God say living in the desert is better than living with a quarrelsome and complaining woman?

Transparency #57

Teacher Note: For a more in-depth understanding of the importance of seeking a woman with a quiet and gentle spirit, read the paragraph "Why Is It Important?" on page 134 of the discussion manual to your students.

Supporting Verse:

  Proverbs 12:4

  C. Is she an industrious woman?

Teacher Note: Point out that a godly woman being able to do the daily duties is important. The tremendous pressure in today's society belittles those industrious qualities by saying they are demeaning to a woman. This type of criticism is not supported by God's Word.

Key Verses:

Proverbs 31:13-16

Key Questions:

1. What qualities from this passage apply to a modern day wife?
2. How can high school girls begin to learn these qualities now?

Supporting Verse:

Proverbs 14:1

Key Questions:

1. Why does a foolish woman tend to tear down her own house?
2. In what ways can she tear down her house?

Wrap Up/Conclusion:

As you conclude this series on dating, stress these two principles:

1. God is concerned that you find the right person to date and marry.
2. God wants you to be a person with the right qualities, so someone would want to date and marry you.

After clarifying these principles, challenge your students to pray them out before God. Also, ask them to pray that God will lead them to the right person with the right qualities.

LOVE vs. INFATUATION
Lesson 21
Part 1 of Chapter 8
(pages 139-145)

Introduction:

There is no time when feelings are more important than during the adolescent years. Nothing stirs up emotions more than when a high school guy or girl thinks he/she is in love. Many times this "love" is only infatuation. And many times their feelings contradict God's instruction on feelings and love.

During this lesson, you as a teacher and friend will be helping your students realize the wisdom and objectivity of God's Word in the area of love. Your students need to understand that feelings are wonderful, but unless we are under control of the Holy Spirit feelings can be our worst enemy. (For a good teaching reference on feelings see Proverbs 4:28.) Most Christian students do not understand the difference between love and infatuation; therefore, they are confused about their dating relationship. Some students do not use objectivity while dating and making crucial decisions (sex before marriage, hasty engagement, pre-mature marriage). Such decisions later lead to a disagreeable marriage and unfulfilled lives.

The following definition will help to clarify infatuation. You may want to write it on an overhead projector or blackboard:

> Infatuation is the emotional impulse of love, based on superficial knowledge of the other person. It has not faced the important tests of time and circumstance.

Transparency #58
Transparency #59

Teacher Note: At the top of page 141 in the discussion manual is a paragraph on the world's view of love. Discuss this concept with your class and ask the following questions.

1. Are there television or magazine advertisements which use the infatuation view of love?
2. What movies contain attractive relationships based on infatuation?
3. Are there popular songs that communicate the infatuation viewpoint?
4. How does the world's view of infatuation love differ from God's view of true maritial love?

(Answer: Christians should have emotional love toward others. But Christian love is not centered on emotions or feelings, but on an act of the will in response to an intellectual evaluation. Christian love is not based on lust, which comes from selfishness, but is other-centered.)

Special Note: Be sure to stress that an infatuation view of love may be only temporary and not a sufficient foundation for a relationship, but the possibility exists that a genuine love relationship could begin with infatuation.

Key Principle:

1. Love is patient.

Teacher Note: Each characteristic of love from 1 Corinthians 13 has been presented as a key principle for this series. The differences between infatuation and love have been applied to real life situations in each key principle.

Key Principle:

Love is patient. Infatuation hurries to become more involved romantically, so the intense feelings may be kept alive. Infatuation tries to change life-styles into our own stereotypes.

Key Verse:

1 Corinthians 13:4

A. The "Big Hurry" Syndrome

Key Questions:

1. Why are people, who are infatuated, in a big rush for:

    * security (assurance that the other person will not leave)?
    * acceptance (being accepted just the way they are)?
    * affection (an aroused feeling of intimacy due to sexual activity)?
    * adventure (seeking new experiences together)?

2. What can be the big problem in rushing into a dating relationship?

    The "Big Hurry" Syndrome is manifested by:

    * boredom in a relationship because of experiencing too much, too fast.
    * saying emphatic things from explosive emotions, before the emotions settle down.
    * leading to frustration because the relationship is going nowhere.
    * saying things not really meant, not based on fact.

Supporting Verse:

Proverbs 18:13

Teacher Note: Share with your students that every relationship needs time to grow, in order to understand and know the other person well. Then ask your class this question and encourage open discussion.

   Someone once said, "If you really want to know if you are in love, time will be your best friend." Is this true? Why? Why not?

Project:

Instruct your students to close their discussion manuals. Tell them that they are to answer the following questions you ask as if they were getting married in six months. Have them tell you why each question is important as they look to marriage.

1. Does your fiance know every side of your personality or just one?
2. How does your fiance react under pressure? (If you marry, your relationship will have <u>more</u> pressure not less.)
3. Is your fiance orderly or sloppy? (This is more important in marriage than you think.)
4. How does your fiance respond to his/her parents? (The attitude toward parents can affect attitude toward you.)
5. Does your fiance make good conversation or can you trust his/her silence to sustain you? (REMEMBER, BOREDOM IS A BIG PROBLEM FACING MODERN MARRIAGES.)
6. Is your fiance lazy or hardworking?
7. Can your relationship last without sexual activity? (Never trust sex to be positive if you experiment pre-maritally. Sex will never keep a relationship going.)
8. What does your fiance think about God? (Good looks and personality won't help develop a better walk with God.)

Teacher Note: Stress to your students that they should take time to know all of these answers no matter what kind of a relationship they have now. Assure them that if they do attempt to find these answers, they will be further ahead than most people going into marriage.

    B. Infatuation tries to change the personality of the partner into our own stereotype.

Transparency #60

Teacher Note: Emphasize that we should discern the characteristics of the person we want to marry, but we cannot force them into a preconceived stereotype.

Application:

You will have to list the following characteristics on an overhead projector or blackboard, or type them out and make copies for each student.

The following are areas where an infatuated person will not be too patient:

- too talkative
- too quiet
- seldom punctual
- lazy

- dominant
- indecisive
- self-centered
- fickle

- jealous
- over sensitive
- impatient
- stubborn

A person who truly loves the other person and discerns after much time that God wants them to continue dating, will be more likely to be patient in these areas.

Teacher Note: *After pointing out these areas of weaknesses for an impatient person, stress that we cannot change anyone through our own efforts. If we try to change them, we automatically put them on a performance test, which produces negative reactions by them. The only positive change that can come about in your partner's life is through submission to the work of the Holy Spirit.*

Project:

Hand out a sheet of paper to each student. Ask your students to give an answer to the following statement.

Could you say to your partner, "I'd be willing to live with you the rest of your life even when:

- *you look good; you look bad?"*
- *you move as quickly as I like; when you move too slowly?"*
- *you smell good; you smell bad?"*
- *you are in a good mood; you are irritated?"*
- *you are on time; you are late?"*
- *you are self-motivated; you are lazy?"*
- *you are sensitive; you are insensitive?"*
- *you are giving; you are selfish?"*
- *you are fun to be with; you are a drag?"*

Wrap Up/Conclusion:

Challenge your students to pray that God will give them the wisdom to discern between infatuation and love in their date life. Also pray that God will help them to be patient with the person they date and to encourage the other person to change negative characteristics in the power of the Holy Spirit.

LOVE vs. INFATUATION
Lesson 22
Part 2 of Chapter 8
(pages 146-148)

Introduction/Review:

Since so many new ideas were introduced in the last lesson you need to conduct a thorough review. Here are some key questions to ask your students in reviewing:

* Why do we need to put God's counsel over our emotions?
* What is infatuation?
* What is true marital love?
* Why are people who are infatuated in such an emotional rush?
* Why is time an important friend to people who are in love?
* What are some probing questions to ask about someone whom you are seriousl dating?
* What happens when you put someone on a performance test in a dating relationship?

Key Principles:

1. Infatuation tends to quickly forget the importance of doing kind deeds for the partner. Genuine love will prove itself through continued, creative service to the partner.
2. Infatuation is easily threatened; therefore, it is possessive and insecure. Genuine love allows freedom for the partner to grow outside of the relationship.

Key Principle 1:

Infatuation tends to quickly forget the importance of doing kind deeds for the partner. Genuine love will prove itself through continued, creative service to the partner

Key Verse:

1 Corinthians 13:4

Teacher Note: Stress that in infatuation people begin giving kind deeds to each other, but soon boredom sets in, and the giving of kindness becomes sporadic or non-existent. On the other hand, a loving relationship gives consistently over a long period of time. Infatuation ends up sporadic because true love is hard work.

Illustration:

Give an example from your life when someone gave you kindness over a period of time. If you cannot think of a boyfriend/girlfriend or husband/wife, tell of *a close friend, mother, father, brother, sister or some other relative who gave consistently in the details of your life.*

Key Questions:

1. *If you are dating now, what activities do you do together? (Besides making out.)*
2. *What projects could you plan together to help both of you grow?*

Project:

Divide your class into teams of twos, one guy and one girl. It you do not have an equal ratio of guys to girls, divide them into teams of three, with at least one girl and one guy per group. Give each team a blank sheet of paper. Have the teams draw a line down the middle of the paper, top to bottom. At the top left hand side, head the column "Attitudes." On the opposite side, head the column "Actions." Under each category, have the teams list the attitudes they would like to have, and the actions they would like to do together. Spend no more than ten minutes on this project.

An example:

ATTITUDES	ACTIONS
1. Supportive	1. Help me with the Word
2. Gentleness	2. Be a good listener
3. Helpful	3. Play tennis

After the project is completed, tell your students that what they have been discussing takes hard work. And, when people get married, the hard work must continue if the relationship is to have meaning.

Key Principle 2:

Infatuation is easily threatened; therefore, it is possessive and insecure. Genuine love allows freedom for the partner to grow outside of the relationship.

Transparency #61

Key Verses:

1 Corinthians 13:4
Proverbs 27:4

Teacher Note: *Jealousy is perhaps one of the biggest problems between two infatuated people. That is why you should be clear in teaching this key principle. Become familiar with the paragraph under "Love is Not Jealous" on page 147 of the discussion manual.*

Key Questions:

1. In Proverbs 27:4, why is jealousy more dangerous and cruel than anger?
2. Can you think of a time when you were extremely jealous?
3. What are some signs of jealousy?
4. How did you feel when you found out that the person you were dating was possessive of you and your time?

Teacher Note: Now, state that while a couple should spend time together, they also need to have other relationships which will help them grow. Clarify that this is healthy and natural for their own relationships. To make this point more vivid, ask these questions.

* Why do some high school couples spend almost all their time together without being with other couples or groups of students?
* What can be some negative results when two people do not spend time with other people of the opposite sex?
* Why does true love allow the other partner the freedom to develop relationships with other people?

Teacher Note: Here are some statements students should be able to say to their dating partner in order to allow their relationship freedom to grow.

- You need to be involved in some hobbies and activities without me.
- You need to spend some nights with your family.
- You need to spend some time with your other friends.
- You need time alone, to think, read or write, without me.
- You need to build your relationship with God, apart from involvement with me.

Also explain that a boyfriend or girlfriend is not their possession, but a gift from God. God desires that they, by serving their partner, encourage that partner to be the most dynamic, positive Christian possible.

Wrap Up/Conclusion:

Challenge your students to return for the next lesson, because it will cover some of the deeper aspects of love. They will not want to miss it. Also, encourage them to prepare for the lesson by reading the material and looking up the verses that correlate. They need to bring their manuals to each session for the best possible learning and discussion.

LOVE vs. INFATUATION
Lesson 23

Part 3 of Chapter 8
(pages 148-152)

Introduction:

In order to prepare your students for the depth and sensitivity they may encounter while discussing this lesson, point out that love is not always roses, smiles and a warm feeling, but is hard work. Tell them that they must face the reality of love bravely in order to survive.

Key Principles:

1. Infatuation finds scrutiny and disagreement hard to accept because it is based on emotion. Love, on the other hand, does not romanticize life's situations, but faces them realistically.
2. Love does not seek to fulfill itself. Infatuation deceives one into believing that the dating partner's needs are being met, when actually his own selfish needs are being fulfilled.

Key Principle 1:

Infatuation finds scrutiny and disagreement hard to accept because it is based on emotion. Love, on the other hand, does not romanticize life's situations, but faces them realistically.

Teacher Note: The infatuated person views true love unrealistically and fears losing the intense feeling. Whenever fear is in a relationship, there is not a mature level of love.

Supporting Verses:

1 John 4:18,19

Key Questions:

1. Are there weaknesses in your life that you keep from your partner, fearing if he/she found out your relationship would end?
2. Are there other things you would like to do, but fear sharing them with your partner?
3. Are there "controversial subjects" you avoid for fear of causing an argument?
4. Does your partner have weaknesses that you want to discuss, but are afraid of getting him/her mad?
5. Are there certain weaknesses which permeate your relationship, but you are afraid to mention them because the relationship might be lost?
6. What are some of those weaknesses?

7. What are some things you would like to do, but won't because of your partner?

Answers:

2. Date others, spend less time with your partner, spend more time with each others' parents, try new hobbies together.
3. Spiritual issues, political opinions.
4. Problems with authority, not treating you with respect, not sensitive to your needs, acts too immature in public, bad body hygiene.
5. Too physical, not enough communication, lack of emphasis on spiritual growth together and individually, too much time together.

Teacher Note: Another way your students can discern whether their relationship is based on love or infatuation, is how it deals with disagreement.

Key Question:

1. How do you react when you have a disagreement with someone?

(Answer: See bottom of page 149 of discussion manual for typical high school student responses.)

Project:

"Role Playing"

For this project select four students, two guys and two girls, to role play different parts. The idea of this project is to exercise communication skills in inter-personal problem solving. Each couple will have their own problem solving task. Encourage the students to be as creative as possible in their roles.

Before the role playing begins, list the following communication skills on an overhead transparency or a blackboard.

1. Always approach the other person with the problem, by saying something positive. (e.g. "You really are sensitive to my needs, but...")
2. Never make a blatant accusation, but take the blame yourself. (e.g. "I should have seen that you needed help, instead I let you...")
3. Avoid threatening the other person. (e.g. "If you don't change your attitude, I'm breaking up with you!")
4. Avoid raising your voice. (e.g. "QUIT YELLING, AND LISTEN TO ME!!")

Type out each role's description so each student has his own to refer to. Or read each role description to the role playing student without the other partner or class knowing what's coming.

PROBLEM SOLVING TASKS:

Couple #1: Guy feels girl wants to spend too much time with him.

Guy's Part: You feel that your girl is spending too much time with you. You really enjoy being with her and want to keep her as a steady date. But, she does take up your time practicing sports, time with your family and other friends, and studying time. You need to convince her that you need more time to do other things.

Girl's Part: You really _like_ your boyfriend, and you believe that your relationship could turn into something strong and serious. You feel that both of you need more time together so your relationship can grow.

Couple #2: Girl feels that the dating relationship is too physical.

Girl's Part: You believe that your boyfriend has been over-aggressive with you physically. You want to stop your physical relationship before it goes too far. You really like him, but something has to be done soon. Convince him that he needs to stop being so aggressive with you physically, and you both need to emphasize your spiritual growth together.

Guy's Part: You really like your girlfriend. In fact, you think you're in love with her. You enjoy being with her, especially alone.

Perhaps you would want to perform two different skits with each couple. For instance, a before-and-after series, showing the differences of not using the communication skills and exercising the skills in a problem solving situation. If you don't have the time to perform both, be sure to use the skills in the role play.

Transparency #62

Key Question:

1. How can a couple grow when facing difficult times?

(Answer: Develop patience, compassion, problem solving skills, respect strengthened love, depend on the Lord, know each other better.)

Teacher Note: Point out that every couple ought to have a "Loving Contest" going on between themselves. The contest entails: "I would like to have more compassion and understanding for your weaknesses than you have for my weaknesses."

Key Principle 2:

Love does not seek to fulfill itself. Infatuation deceives one into believing that the dating partner's needs are being met, when actually his own selfish needs are being fulfilled.

Key Verse:

1 Corinthians 13:5

Supporting Verse:

Acts 20:35

Transparency #63

Teacher Note: Stress to your students that having their emotional needs met in a dating relationship is okay, but that fulfilling one's own needs is a by-product of meeting the other person's needs first. Explain to your girls how they can become confused about using a guy for their own selfish needs, as opposed to placing his needs first.

To test the true motives of your girls for wanting to get married, ask the following five questions. Cover these questions with your class and lead into open discussion on giving in a relationship.

1. Regardless of the mood of my marriage partner, would I be willing to give up half of my own time to be with him/her?
2. Would I be willing to give even more time if we had a child?
3. Am I willing to give up the majority of my independence?
4. Am I willing to give up my earned money for my family?
5. Am I willing to be vulnerable to heartbreak? (Remember, love is demanding).

Teacher Note: Because guys tend to fall in love with a girl's good looks and body, you need to point out that a girl's physical appearance will not hold a marriage together.

Ask your guys the following questions in order to discern their attitudes towards the physical attraction of a dating or marriage partner. Encourage discussion.

1. If a good body is such an important ingredient in marriage, why are there so many divorces in Hollywood?
2. Do you think your wife's good looks will hold the relationship together through trying times?
3. If you become upset with her, will her good looks quiet your anger?
4. Does your girlfriend appreciate a compliment more for her good looks, or for her personality?
5. If your girlfriend was left physically scarred from an accident, would you still be able to tell her that you love her?
6. Would you get bored if you had to spend hours talking to her on the phone rather than seeing her?
7. If good looks are so important and lasting, why are we constantly trying to improve our looks?

Supporting Verses:

2 Corinthians 4:16-18

Wrap Up/Conclusion:

Conclude this series on "Love vs Infatuation" by telling your students that the second most important decision they will make is who they choose to marry. Since this is true, they need to apply Proverbs 3:5,6 to their expectations of real love. Challenge them to pray, right now, for God's wisdom in knowing the difference between love and infatuation.

CLEARING THE MIND
Lesson 24
Part 1 of Chapter 9
(pages 155-159)

Sr. H
May, 1981

Transparency #64

Introduction:

In the next two lessons you will be teaching and discussing the power of the mind in the Christian life. Most Christian high school students do not understand the importance of their thought life nor how to meditate on God's Word. These lessons may not be exciting to your students, but they are just as important.

As you introduce this lesson, stress that God is aware of our thoughts and He is very concerned about what we think. (See Psalms 139:2) The reason why God is so concerned about our thoughts is because we eventually become what we think. (See Proverbs 23:7) God knows that the battlefield of allegiance, whether for God or for Satan, lies with our minds.

Since most students don't spend time dwelling on their thoughts, ask the following questions to provoke their thinking on thinking. The questions are also found on page 156 of the discussion manual.

For the fifth question have your students write "none," "a little," "some," or "much" next to each subject.

1. What fraction of your thinking would fall into the category of worry?
2. What thoughts occupy your mind as you go to sleep?
3. What thoughts come to you first thing in the morning?
4. What fraction of your thoughts are impure?
5. How much time do you spend thinking about:

   *your job   *your car   *your boy/girlfriend
   *your sister   *your brother   *the Friday night date
   *homework   *parents   *athletics
   *sex   *yourself   *club activities
   *clothes   *your sin   *grades
   *God

Teacher Note: Remind your students that God's goal is for all of our thoughts to be obedient to Him. See 2 Corinthians 10:5. This verse does not mean that every thought has to be on Christ, but that we have thoughts showing our obedience to Christ. We should be willing to let God test all of our thoughts and allow Him to expose those thoughts which are not pleasing to Him. (See Psalm 119:23-24)

Key Principle:

1. The three principle antagonists waging war on our minds are Satan, the world, and the flesh.

Key Verses:

   2 Corinthians 11:3
   Romans 12:2
   Romans 8:6

A. Satan and his demonic helpers are out to mess up our thinking.

Transparency #65

Key Verse:

2 Corinthians 11:3

Key Questions:

1. According to this verse, what is Satan's goal for our mind?
2. What are some techniques he used to play on Eve's mind? (see Genesis 3:1-5)

   (Answer: Put doubt in her mind, misrepresented God's loving intentions, lied to her.)

Teacher Note: Explain to your students that Satan has one goal for our thinking-- to get us to think on <u>anything</u> other than Christ pleasing thoughts. Satan and his demons are very subtle and crafty to get our minds on wrong things, like worry, fear, guilt, doubt and despair. Satan also gets us to think too much about seemingly good things--so that these good things become bad when dwelled upon in excess--subjects like sports, love life, jobs, friends, future, and past. common for our minds to wonder on more than necessary.

Supporting Verse:

Ephesians 6:11

B. The world bombards our minds with all kind of wrong thoughts.

Transparency #66

Key Verse:

Romans 12:2

Key Questions:

1. Does God want us to think like non-Christians, according to Romans 12:2?
2. What are some outside sources that bombard your minds?

   (Answer: Teachers, unsaved friends, newspaper, radio, TV, magazines, records, movies.)

3. What is the basic message the world tells us?

   (Answer: All that matters is ourselves and the temporary things rather than doing God's will.)

Project:

Give a sheet of paper to each student and ask them to write down three advertising jingles or slogans. Next, have them write down two or three lines from a rock song that is two months old or younger. After they have completed their writing, ask them to write one Bible verse they have memorized during the last two months. This exercise should prove the amount of stimuli that can control their thoughts--whether from the world or from God's Word.

Teacher Note: The average high school student listens to almost 30 hours of radio a week and watches 28 hours of television. The amount of stimuli they receive is amazing. However, God does not expect people to escape the world. See John 17:15. God does have a plan to combat the thoughts thrust upon us by the world, the flesh, and Satan.

C. Our minds are attacked by our own sin nature.

Key Verse:

Romans 8:6

Teacher Note: Explain to your students that each of us has a rebellious nature towards God. Our sin nature is also called the flesh, which quickly throws wrong thoughts into our minds.

Key Questions:

1. What is your first thought when someone makes fun of you?
2. What is your first thought when someone hits you?
3. What is your first thought when someone tells a funny story that's dirty?
4. What is your first thought when something does not go your way?
5. What is your first thought when your parents discipline you?
6. What is your first thought when your teacher does not give you the grade you thought you deserved?
7. What is your first thought when your best friend dates someone you want to date?

(Answer: Point out that the first thoughts that come to mind are not the thoughts God wants us to have, because our sin nature is quick to react.)

Teacher Note: Be sure to clarify that the wrong thoughts that jump quickly into our heads is not sin. God says we sin when we meditate or entertain the thoughts and carry out those wrong thoughts.

Illustration:

On page 159 of the discussion manual is an illustrated chart of Philippians 4:8. The chart features a list of thoughts God wants us to harbor as contrasted with our natural thoughts. Discuss this chart thoroughly and add any of your own examples to clarify it.

Wrap Up/Conclusion:

Remind your students that a big war is taking place all around them for their minds. They are being attacked from all sides by the world, the devil and their own sin nature. But, God tells them they can have victory in their thought life.
Inform them that the next lesson shares what God's secret is for a victorious thought life.
Close today's lesson by challenging your students to pray for discernment in the differences between godly thoughts and thoughts that lead to sin.

CLEARING THE MIND
Lesson 25
Part 2 of Chapter 9
(pages 161-166)

ST, HA May 1981

Introduction/Review:

In reviewing the last lesson, you need to point out that a fierce battle is taking place for your students' minds. The devil, the world and their own rebellious natures are working together to destroy their thinking.

Share with your class that God says they can have a good thought life, one that pleases Him. He actually gives them His plan on how to achieve one in His power. In this lesson you will be teaching your class God's plan for a healthy way of thinking.

Key Principles:

1. Part of the way to have a clean and powerful thought life is to think about Jesus Christ.
2. Another way to renew our minds is to meditate on God's Word.
3. Renewing our minds through meditation on God's Word will help give us victory over sin, great wisdom and prosperity.

Key Principle 1:

Part of the way to have a clean and powerful thought life is to think about Jesus Christ.

Transparency #67

Teacher Note: Most of your students do not understand what a renewed mind means. A renewed mind is a mind that God has healed, changed and made right, so that a rebellious life style is changed into a life style pleasing to God. A renewed mind can stand before a holy God in confidence knowing that it is thinking godly thoughts.

Key Verse:

Romans 12:2

Supporting Verse:

Psalm 19:14

Key Questions:

1. According to Romans 12:2, what is God's solution to the problem of our unclean minds?
2. What does "renewing the mind" mean?
3. How often do we need to renew our minds?

   (Answer: Since we are constantly having negative stimulus thrust upon our minds by the flesh, the world and Satan, we need to be in the Word everyday.)

Project:

Take about 15 minutes to complete this project. It will help your students think more about Jesus Christ. Each student will need one 3"x5" card. Have each student read Mark 10:46-52 three times to become very familiar with it. Answer these questions about Mark 10:46-52:

1. How did Jesus respond to the people around Him?
2. In what ways was He sensitive to the blind man's need?
3. How would you appraise Christ's conduct?
4. How were the words He spoke appropriate to the need of the moment?
5. What was the result of Christ's work?

Compare your conduct and attitude to Christ's:

1. How could your attitudes become more like Christ's attitudes.
2. What situation might you face today that will allow you to respond the way Christ responded?

Write on the 3" x 5" card:

- The attributes of Christ that you could apply to the situation you might face today.

Now, let these thoughts of Christ and His actions continually dominate <u>your</u> mind and actions. As you apply this project day after day, a change in <u>your</u> thought life will result.

Key Principle 2:

Another way to renew our minds is to meditate on God's Word.

Teacher Note: You may wish to define meditation. Strictly speaking, meditation means to mull over God's Word in our minds. Meditating is our personal devotion and discipline to a deep, continual reflection on God and His Word. It involves the daily dwelling of our thoughts upon God's Word.

Transparency #68

Supporting Verses:

> Deuteronomy 6:6,7
> Psalm 1:2

Illustration:

On the top of page 163 of the discussion manual, Deuteronomy 6:6-7 is illustrated specifically for the high school student. The chart is entitled "When to Meditate." Please teach this chart to your students carefully and clearly. (If your students do not have their own copies of the discussion manual, copy this chart on an overhead projector or blackboard.)

Key Question:

1. When would be the best time, each day, for you to focus all of your attention on God and His Word?

Key Principle 3:

Renewing our minds through meditation on God's Word will help give us victory over sin, great wisdom, and prosperity.

    A. Victory over Sin

Key Verses:

> Psalm 119:9-11

Teacher Note: Stress that there are no short cuts to developing pure thoughts. After so much stimulus for unclean, negative thinking, God's Word takes time to penetrate and clean up our minds. Only God's Word through the work of the Holy Spirit can accomplish a pure mind.

Key Question:

1. How can you store God's Word in your heart?

Illustration:

King David had a good reason for thinking bitter and anxious thoughts. People were slandering him with false accusations. It would have been easy for David to lie in bed and fret long into the night, allowing thoughts of revenge to captivate his mind. But he did just the opposite. (See Psalm 119:78)

    B. Great Wisdom

Key Verses:

    Psalm 119:97-100

Key Questions:

1. According to Psalm 119:97-100, God's Word will make you wiser than your enemies. Why?
2. Why will the Scriptures make you wiser than your teachers?
3. Why will the Bible make you wiser than older people?

    C. Brings Prosperity

Key Verses:

    Psalm 1:1-3

Key Questions:

1. According to Psalm 1:3, what happens to the work of those who meditate on God's Word?
2. In what areas will God cause you to prosper?

Transparency #69

Wrap Up/Conclusion:

To conclude this lesson and series on "Clearing the Mind," have your students concentrate on Psalm 119:9-11. Command silence as they do this for a minute and a half.

Then, have your students silently pray these verses back to God.

TEMPTATION
Lesson 26
Chapter 10
(pages 169-180)

Introduction:

This final lesson will enable you to help your students see how their sin nature leads them into temptation. Also, your students will begin to grasp how they can resist temptation in the power of the Holy Spirit. Because this lesson will only give you an introduction to temptation, we suggest a more indepth study found in Volume 3 of the <u>Discussion Manual for Student Relationships</u> in the chapter, "How to Break Bad Habits." But, to teach this lesson, you need to thoroughly read the entire chapter, underlining and making notes as you read. Then, teach directly from the discussion manual.

Transparency #70

Teacher Note: Before introducing the key principles, make sure your students understand these three points.

1. Most students are not aware of the spiritual warfare surrounding them.
2. Satan hates us if we are Christians because we have greatly insulted him.
3. Satan is out to destroy our lives and to make us ineffective.

For clearer definitions of "flesh" and "temptation", see page 171 of the discussion manual. The lesson is difficult to teach if you and your students do not agree on the meaning of temptation.

Transparency #71

Key Principles:

1. Our rebellious nature has techniques to lead us into sin.
2. There are five ways we can fight off temptation when it strikes.

Application:

The following are key words and phrases that must be understood by your students before they can effectively learn about temptation. Note that some terms require the appropriate transparency while being discussed. If you do not have the overhead transparencies, try to paint verbal illustrations or give examples of each term.

* Temptation (page 171)
* Flesh (page 171)
* Lust of the Flesh (page 172)
* "Carried-Away" Stage (pages 172 and 173) **Transparency #72 - #75**

* "Enticement" Stage (page 174)   **Transparency #76**
* "Conception" Stage (page 175)
* "Birth-of-Sin" Stage (pages 175 and 176)
* Sin-maturing" Stage (page 176)
* Moral Law" (or "Death") Stage (page 176) Use **Transparency #77**

Key Principle 1:

Our rebellious nature has techniques to lead us into sin.

Key Verses:

James 1:14-16

Teacher Note: In order to fully understand Key Principle 1, analyze James 1:14-16, word by word and phrase by phrase.

Project:

The following is a story you should read to your students to show them how each of the temptation stages are very real in their daily lives. The story may appear brazen, but the authors of this teacher's guide feel that the story portrays a true-to-life situation, and will seem quite realistic to your students.

"THE TEMPTATION OF CHRIS THE CHRISTIAN"

One day Chris the Christian is talking with four of his non-Christian friends. The subject is "girls" at school. During the course of their discussion, the name of Marsha comes up and everybody boasts about how immoral Marsha is with the guys she dates.

Stage 1   Chris has never met Marsha before, but his mind starts stirring on how this girl will respond to him. Of course, he doesn't want to spend a lot of time with Marsha -- he just wants to "get to know" her!

Chris the Christian knows he should spend time with Christian girls, because they will help lead him to a pure life. But he still wants to try it out with Marsha. Besides, she's good looking.

The next day, after school, Chris runs into his good buddy, Immoral Eddie. Chris says, "Hey Eddie, about this Marsha. You know her really well' would you do me a big favor and introduce me to her?" "Sure!" says Eddie, "I just saw her upstairs. Let's go up there now."

Stage 2   As they get upstairs, they both see Marsha at the other end of the hall. Chris says, "Wow! She's lookin' great! Nobody dresses like that around here!"

"You bet," says Eddie. "She's dynamite!"

Eddie introduces Chris to Marsha, and right away she acts very interested in Chris. She tells him that she's been noticing him, and begins acting very friendly toward him. Somehow, Chris gets away from the enticing conversation with Marsha.

Stage 3   *For the next two days, all that's on Chris' mind is going out with Marsha. He knows if they go out on a date, he could easily get involved with her. His mind keeps trying to convince him that he has to go out with her to see what he could do with a girl like Marsha.*

Two nights after their meeting, Chris is standing by the phone at home. He's struggling to decide if he should ask her out or forget about her altogether. Deep in his heart, Chris knows he shouldn't call her, but his strong sin nature convinces him that he must try. Chris picks up the phone and dials her number. He gets a date for Friday night.

Stage 4   *Friday night finally rolls around, and Chris and Marsha go out. Later in the date, they park and begin to "make out". Soon they go too far physically.*

The next day, Chris realizes he has sinned, but he enjoyed being with Marsha so much that he asks her out again for next Friday night.

Stage 5   *Chris and Marsha begin going out again and again. But, each date takes them a little further physically.*

Finally, on the ninth date, they go all the way! Soon Chris becomes very guilty and starts feeling like a slave to his sexual desires. He knows he's sinned, so he begins to get down on himself for what he's done. Plus, he constantly worries about his reputation at school. He worries that the news of his sin will get around to other Christians who know him. And there's always the chance of

Stage 6   *getting Marsha pregnant. After only one more date with Marsha, she drops him. Because he's spent so much time with Marsha, he's quit going to activities at church and feels alienated from his Christian friends. For days Chris is left in limbo. Dropped by Marsha and out of fellowship with his Christian friends, Chris wastes a lot of time daydreaming and uninvolved.*

Finally, Chris gives up and goes to his youth leader at church. He tells his youth leader that several days ago he had an accident with a girl on a date.

Teacher, after you have read through the story, ask your class this question:

"Did Chris really have an accident?" Allow a little time to discuss various answers. Now, reread the story aloud, but this time, have your students stop you when they recognize each stage of temptation.

Transition:

God does not intend for us to live a wrong existence with guilt feelings, slavery to sins, low self-worth, worry, broken relationships or wasting time. We can be faked out by sin as something that leads to a good existence with God. Fortunately, God has a remedy when temptation strikes.

Key Principle 2:

There are five ways we can fight off temptation when it strikes.

Teacher Note: *Perhaps the best way to teach these five remedies of overcoming temptation is to list each one on an overhead transparency or blackboard.*

A. *Recognize the plan of attack.*

Key Verses:

    1 Peter 5:8
    James 1:13,14
    1 John 2:16

Teacher Note: *We are attacked through temptation everyday by three sources:*

    the devil -- 1 Peter 5:8
    the world -- 1 John 2:16
    our sin nature -- James 1:13,14

But the first way to combat temptation is to identify which of these three sources it is coming from.

Transparency #78

Application:

When temptation hits you, ask yourself, "What stage of temptation am I in -- the curiosity stage, enticement stage, or what?" Fleeing temptation is easier if you are in one of the earlier stages than if you're waist deep in sin. Half of the battle against temptation is being aware of the source and its techniques.

B. *Recognize that you are incapable of facing and conquering a temptation in your own strength. You must know that the key to victory is in the power of the Holy Spirit working through you.*

Key Verse:

    Galatians 5:16

Application:

When you encounter temptation, pray something like this:

"God, my sin nature is acting up again. I know that there is nothing good in me. I can't get out of this situation on my own. Help me flee by filling me with your Holy Spirit. Thank you, Lord, for hearing me."

C. *When you face temptation caused by youthful lust, <u>FLEE</u> -- get out of there as fast as you can!*

Key Verse:

    2 Timothy 2:22

Key Question:

1. What does it mean to "flee?"

    (Answer: To flee means never to argue with the flesh or give it an inch to grasp on a situation, because the flesh has a deceptive power too great for us. The desire to sin can become so intense that our ability to reason is overridden by our emotions. At this point, run as fast as you can away from the temptation and think about it later.)

D. Realize that a key to conquering temptation is to be around friends who really love Christ.

Key Verse:

2 Timothy 2:22

Supporting Verse:

James 5:16

Key Questions:

1. What attribute should we be striving for as we spend time with friends?
2. How can Christian friends help you face temptation?
3. Who are some people you know who would help you be more like Christ?

E. Recognize the positive results of being obedient to God.

Key Verse:

James 1:17

Key Questions:

1. Is it logical that God would give bad gifts to those who obey Him?
2. What are the positive results of obeying God?

    (Answer: A clear conscience, a greater respect for yourself, genuine inner contentment, fulfillment, lack of worry, hope for future.)

3. What are the consequences of disobeying God?

    (Answer: See stage #6)

Wrap Up/Conclusion:

Challenge your students to decide in their own minds between compromising their Christianity by allowing temptation to lead them to pleasurable sins, and walking with God by depending on His Holy Spirit to lead them away from temptation. Explain that if they choose to let sin continue in their lives, it will only cause them more heartache. But, obedience to God will give them more joy than all of the pleasurable sins they can think of.

Close this lesson by praying that each student may have the desire to resist temptation, and that they will know how to apply the steps presented in this lesson.

Further reading from Shepherd Productions

DISCUSSION MANUAL FOR STUDENT DISCIPLESHIP is a quality tool for discipling the young Christian. Basic elements for solid spiritual growth are included like God's Love and Forgiveness, Trials, the Word, Your Prayers, the Spirit Filled Life, Fellowship and more. The manual was designed with simplicity to encourage any person discipling a young believer to read and share on a one-on-one basis. Three indepth quiet time studies are included at the end of each chapter.   paper $6.95

DISCUSSION MANUAL FOR STUDENT RELATIONSHIPS, VOLUME 2 presents more gut-level topics in the same dynamic style as Volume 1. Covering some of life's most puzzling issues like How to Glorify God, What is Love, What Love is Not, Peer Group Pressure, Honesty, Facing Death and many more. This manual is a must for every youth library and a resource for every youth worker. paper $7.95

DISCUSSION MANUAL FOR STUDENT RELATIONSHIPS, VOLUME 3 provides more right-on issues facing today's youth in the practical tradition of Volumes 1 and 2. This manual deals with Cliques, Broken Homes, Drugs and Alcohol, Breaking Bad Habits, Rock Music and more. These are topics seldom found in other youth materials, making Volumes 1, 2 and 3 exceptional in their own way. paper $7.95

CASSETTE TAPES FROM SHEPHERD PRODUCTIONS: Correlated cassette tapes are available for many of the chapters from the manuals. The tapes feature Dawson McAllister speaking to students at the Student Relationships Conferences. These tapes make excellent resources for lesson preparation or for youth group listening. each tape $3.50

Today more than ever before students are asking the questions, — "Is Christianity practical?" "What will it do for me?"

The following series of manuals deal with God's answers to students' needs in a practical way.

CHAPTER TITLE

Discussion Manual for Student Discipleship
Written by Dawson McAllister and Dan Webster

DESCRIPTION

Chapter Title	Description
The Importance of Your New Life	This chapter deals with our newly established relationship with God through Jesus.
The Importance of God's Love and Forgiveness	Learning to deal with sin on a daily basis and understanding the completeness of God's forgiveness is discussed in this section.
The Importance of Your Trials	Understanding trials, why we have them, and how God uses them are the topics in this chapter.
The Importance of The Word	This important section reaffirms the importance and reliability of God's Word in the believers life.
The Importance of Your Quiet Time	Spending time daily in God's Word is essential to spiritual growth. Practical "how to's" are given in this chapter.
The Importance of Your Prayer	A scriptural and motivational basis for prayer is discussed in this chapter.
The Importance of the Spirit-Filled Life	The key to this section is its simplicity in answering the questions--Who is the Holy Spirit? Why did He come? What is His role?
The Importance of Walking in the Spirit	How to allow God Himself to live His life through us on a daily basis is discussed in this section.
The Importance of Your Fellowship	This chapter explains the importance of the Christian student spending time with other Christians.
The Importance of Sharing Your Faith	The goal of this chapter is to introduce students to the joy and excitement of introducing others to Jesus Christ and motivate them in a positive way to witness.

CHAPTER TITLE

DESCRIPTION

The Importance of Obedience • • • • • • This chapter deals with our **responsibility** to God in regard to our living a successful Christian life.

Learning to Obey God • • • • • • • • This continues the theme of chapter 1, with specific application concerning our being obedient.

Worship • • • • • • • • • • • The importance of worship as a lifestyle is discussed here.

The Christian and the
Lordship of Christ • • • • • • • • • This chapter is the very essence of the Christian life. Learning to let Christ be Lord is the key to a successful lifestyle.

The Christian Life and
Endurance • • • • • • • • • • Many Christians start out in a blaze of glory but end in disaster. This chapter deals with the Christian and endurance.

The Responsibility of Love • • • • • Learning to love one another in Christ is dealt with in this chapter.

Our Responsibility Toward
Other Christians • • • • • • • • • The importance of our relationships with other Christians is discussed here.

How to Start Your Own
Ministry. • • • • • • • • • • • Jesus taught us not to only hear His words. This chapter gives helpful and creative ways of starting your own ministry.

CHAPTER TITLE

DESCRIPTION

The Importance of Understanding
The Bible, A Counselling Book
— The value and wisdom the Bible can shed on everyday life is discussed here.

The Importance of Knowing
God's Will
— Whom should I marry? What school should I attend? What vocation should I pursue? are questions this chapter will help answer.

The Importance of a Balanced
Self-Image
— This chapter shares how God sees us and how to form a proper self-image.

The Importance of Dealing
with Loneliness
— One of the biggest problems the American student faces is loneliness. This chapter gives answers on how to deal with this problem.

The Importance of Understanding
Parents
— Few relationships affect our lives as do our relationship with our parents. The problems and solutions are shared in this chapter.

The Importance of Understanding
Sex
— This section deals with the rationale of why God's saying what He does about sex.

The Importance of Understanding
Dating
— This chapter gives insight into questions such as--What are the problems in dating? What should I look for in a date? Does God have a plan for my date life?

The Importance of Understanding
Love
— This work deals with some of the differences between love and infatuation.

The Importance of Clearing The
Mind
— The importance of thinking pure and Godly thoughts are discussed in this chapter.

The Importance of Dealing With
Temptation
— Being tempted and knowing who tempts us is not always easy to recognize. This chapter gives practical insights in the whole area of temptation.

The New TEACHER'S GUIDE Makes the Discussion Manual Easy and Complete to Teach!

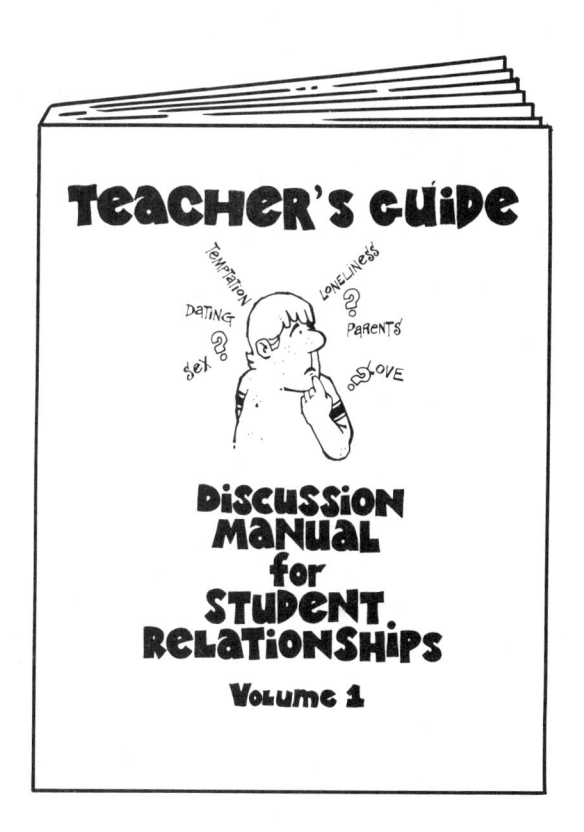

You Get:
- 26 Lessons in Outline Form
- Over 30 Projects
- Additional Bible References
- Hundreds of Questions
- Many Illustrations and Applications
- Lesson Aim and Goals
- Plus, Built-in Teacher Training Tips

Get this comprehensive TEACHER'S GUIDE today!

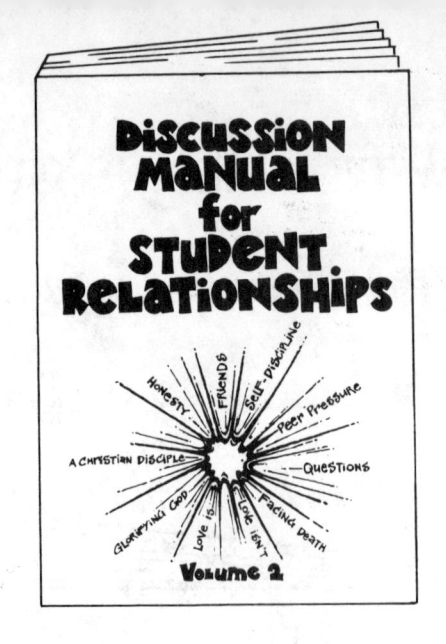

Chapter Title — Description

How to Glorify God — Glorifying God and how to do it can be difficult to understand and teach. This simple chapter gets to the heart of glorifying God.

Discipleship — This chapter shares the answers to the ques What does it mean to be a disciple of Jesus Where do I begin?

Love — Using I Corinthians 13 as its guide this chapter clearly defines what true love is.

What Love Is Not — Again using the love chapter as its basis this chapter explains what love is not.

Questions on Dating — The author of the manual Dawson McAllister, answers questions high school students across the country are asking on dating.

Peer Group Pressure — One of the strongest influences in our lives is the thoughts and actions of our peers towards us. In this discussion we learn how to deal with this pressure.

Making Friends — This chapter stresses the importance of learning how to make friends and the type of friends God desires for us to have.

Honesty — Honesty is often rejected in a world where personal gain is more important than trustworthiness. Here we investigate the results of being dishonest and the benefits of honesty.

This book is a must for the youth library.

Discussion Manual for Student Relationships Vol. 3

CHAPTER TITLE — DESCRIPTION

How To Deal With Cliques — This chapter deals with the ever common problem of cliques in a youth group, what God has to say about cliques and how to deal with bitterness toward the elite.

What To Do When Your Boyfriend Or Girlfriend "Drops You" — Being rejected by someone we date and care about is very difficult to handle. This chapter relates to us dealing with broken hearts.

God's View Of The Misuse Of Drugs And Alcohol — This in depth discussion shares why God is absolutely against the misuse of drugs & alcohol. This work gives a positive answer to the problem -- the person of Jesus Christ.

How To Break Bad Habits — Recognizing bad habits and learning how to break them is the topic of this chapter. Deep and practical truths are explained to the Christian on how to deal with sin.

How To Develop New Healthy Habits — This important section, in a very practical way, helps explain how to begin to form new and healthy habits.

How To Live In A Broken Home — Living in a broken home and allowing God's love to mend some of the hurts isn't easy. This chapter gives some insights into this area.

How To Deal With Guilt — Every student at one time or another faces the emotional pressure of guilt. This sections simply shares how God deals with guilt. This chapter is a must for any youth worker who does counseling.

The Christian Student And Rock Music — The authors give insight into the advantages and disadvantages of listening to rock music and some creative alternatives.

Discipling Your Time — Time is one of the most important commodities we have. This chapter deals with how to make the most of our time.

How to Face Death — One thing we will all experience is death. This chapter answers the questions--What is death? Why is there death? Where does one go when he/she dies?

STUDENT RELATIONSHIPS CONFERENCE
WITH
DAWSON McALLISTER

The goal of Shepherd Productions is to be a servant to the local youth worker in his efforts to disciple and win students to Christ. One of the key ministries of Shepherd Productions is the Student Relationships Conference with Dawson McAllister.

Dawson, a nationally known youth speaker, lectures each night on selected topics dealing with the problems facing the American student and God's answers to those problems. Areas such as loneliness, self image, guilt, bad habits, broken homes, rock music, drugs and alcohol, cliques, peer group pressure, infatuation and others are discussed.

FOR FURTHER INFORMATION, WRITE TO:

SHEPHERD PRODUCTIONS, INC.
P.O. BOX 512
ENGLEWOOD, COLORADO 80151

3294 South Acoma
P.O. Box 512
Englewood, Colorado 80151

SHIP TO:

name _____

street _____

city _____ state _____ zip _____

QUANTITY	MANUALS	CODE	PRICE	TOTAL PRICE
	Discussion Manual for Student Discipleship, Vol. 1	D1	$6.95	$
	Discussion Manual for Student Discipleship, Vol. 2	D2	$6.95	$
	Discussion Manual for Student Relationships, Vol. 1	R1	$7.95	$
	Teacher's Guide, Vol. 1	TR1	$5.95	$
	78 Overhead Transparencies, Vol. 1	OR1	$39.50	$
	Teacher's Set, Vol. 1 (Includes, 1 Student Relationships Manual, 1 Teacher's Guide, 1 Set of 78 Transparencies)	TSR1	$47.50	$
	Discussion Manual for Student Relationships, Vol. 2	R2	$7.95	$
	Discussion Manual for Student Relationships, Vol. 3	R3	$7.95	$

QUANTITY	TAPES	CODE	PRICE	TOTAL PRICE
	Magnificent Messiah (Set)	MMS	$12.00	$
	Man of Sorrows	MM1	$3.50	$
	Six Trials of Jesus	MM2	$3.50	$
	Against All Odds	MM3	$3.50	$
	Isn't He Great	MM4	$3.50	$

Total Column 1 (Add to Column 2) $ _____

QUANTITY	TAPES Con't.	CODE	PRICE	TOTAL PRICE
	God's Answer (Set)	GAS	$19.50	$
	The Bible/God's Will	GA1	$3.50	$
	Self-Esteem/Loneliness	GA2	$3.50	$
	Parents	GA3	$3.50	$
	Students & Sex	GA4	$3.50	$
	Dating	GA5	$3.50	$
	What Real Love Is	GA6	$3.50	$
	Trials and Temptations	GA7	$3.50	$
	Walking By Faith (Set)	WFS	$14.50	$
	What is Faith?	WF1	$3.50	$
	Making a Need for Faith	WF2	$3.50	$
	Abraham and Faith	WF3	$3.50	$
	Noah—Faith & Future	WF4	$3.50	$
	Gideon—Growing Faith	WF5	$3.50	$
	Jesus Series (Set)	JSS	$12.00	$
	Jesus and Peter	JS1	$3.50	$
	Jesus and Pilate	JS2	$3.50	$
	Jesus and Judas	JS3	$3.50	$
	What Christ Thought on the Cross	JS4	$3.50	$
	Love vs. Infatuation	LI	$3.50	$
	Peer Pressure	PP	$3.50	$
	Making Friends	MF	$3.50	$
	How to Deal With a Broken Heart	BH	$3.50	$
	Straight Talk on Love, Sex, & Dating for Girls	ST1	$3.50	$
	Straight Talk on Love, Sex, & Dating for Guys	ST2	$3.50	$

Discount of $1.00 per manual on orders of 20 or more of one manual.

Column 2 Total $ _____
Column 1 Total $ _____
Total Both Columns $ _____
(Colorado residents add 3½% sales tax) $ _____

TOTAL AMOUNT ENCLOSED $ _____
ALL ORDERS FILLED ON A CASH ONLY BASIS.

Have you ordered materials from Shepherd Productions before? Yes ____ No ____